The Establishment:

The Fallen Tent of David and

God's end-time House of Prayer

by J. Scott Husted

Copyright 2004, 2018, J. Scott Husted. All rights reserved.

Scripture taken from the HOLY BIBLE, NEW INTERNATIONAL VERSION®. Copyright © 1973, 1978, 1984 International Bible Society. Used by permission of Zondervan. All rights reserved.

The "NIV" and "New International Version" trademarks are registered in the United States Patent and Trademark Office by International Bible Society. Use of either trademark requires the permission of International Bible Society.

ISBN: 978-0-557-04270-8

To my wife, Dionne, and my son Jonah.

"And I myself will be a *Ring of Fire* around it,' declares the LORD, 'and I will be its glory within.' …"

Zechariah 2:5

What Readers Are Saying:

"Scott Husted's book, 'The Establishment: the fallen tent of David and God's end-time House of Prayer' is powerful because he received his revelation for it the same way David received the pattern for the temple – by waiting on God.

This book contains amazing descriptions of the way earth interacts with heaven through prayer. It is packed with prophetic revelation! This word has got to get out to the body of Christ."

-Wesley and Stacey Campbell, Pastors and prophetic Evangelists, President and Vice President of Revival Now! and Be a Hero Ministries

"'The Establishment' is a great word from a seasoned prophetic intercessor with a call to the establishment of God's end-time mandate for worship, intercession and the prophetic: The House of Prayer. Read it -- and take special note of God's end-time mandate on the Pacific Northwest!"

-Todd Bentley, Evangelist, President of Fresh Fire Ministries International

"Each time I read Scott's writings I feel a sense of urgency for souls and divine strategies to reach and disciple as many as we can, while we can. I also sense great peace and a holy hunger and curiosity to see and listen to what the Holy Spirit is speaking through Scott. He brings a refreshing perspective to the seemingly increasing confusion and darkness we see. He ties together what the Word says and Holy Spirit's breath with great clarity. With fresh revelation and a strong anointing Scott casts God's vision regarding the Ring of Fire and the end-time House of David houses of prayer strategy through worship, intercession and revelation.

-Jorge Parrott Ph.D., President of Eagle Missions International

"'The Establishment: the fallen tent of David and God's end-time House of Prayer' is visionary, challenging and unique. This groundbreaking book left me wanting to don a priest's garb and get a flight ticket to heaven's courts. Not just a one-way ticket, mind you! His book's flight plan has a return leg to the journey. God is ushering in His Son's Kingdom and He won't do it without an empowered priesthood redeemed in Christ.

In this book Scott calls us to the inner counsels of the Most High to discuss and implement His strategies. Personally. He calls us to see the work and the tangible and real benefits of a priestly role in operation, implementing a great Divine Transfer: that the kingdoms of this world are becoming the Kingdoms of our Lord and Christ.

He calls us to a place where actions are initiated by One having authority and power to execute His work. He calls us to partake of the heavenly "board room" where the true "power brokers" convene. He calls us to the heavenly White House and the Oval Office. To a high place of honor in the spirit.

Most importantly, this book is a call to establish outposts on bended knee where humility and authority embrace in the Risen Christ.

I deeply encourage you to consider reading this work. You will be blessed. Not only in the reading, but in the journey that unfolds before you. God bless!"

-**Michael Mooney**, Businessman, Kingdom Business Consultant and Author

"Scott Husted masterfully unfolds the "nuts and bolts" regarding the House of Prayer for these last days. From his personal experiences, right through to the restoration of David's tabernacle and how it applies to the end-time church, it's all there! I highly recommend this enlightening book as a welcome addition to anyone's prayer library."

-**Tom Reed**, House of Prayer Pioneer

Table of Contents

Forward by Jorge Parrott Ph.D.

Author's Forward

Section I - A Call to the House of Prayer

Chapter 1 The Volcanic Chain

Chapter 2 A New Thing

Section II - Foundations of The House of Prayer

Chapter 3 The Three-Strand Cord: God's DNA for the Structure of the House of Prayer

Chapter 4 God's Pattern for the Function of the House of Prayer: The Pattern of Heaven

Chapter 5 The Content of the House of Prayer: A Journey to the Tree of Life

Section III - The Many Faces of the House of Prayer

Chapter 6 The House of Prayer as Bridal Chamber

Chapter 7 The House of Prayer as Strategy Room

Chapter 8 The House of Prayer as Creative Community

Chapter 9 The House of Prayer as Resource Center

Chapter 10 The House of Prayer and Kingdom Enterprise

Chapter 11 David's Heart for the Temple, and God's Heart for the Establishment of the House of Prayer Today

Section IV - Our Story

Chapter 12 Dark Days

Chapter 13 God's Glory in the Nations

Chapter 14 The Glory Continues

Chapter 15 The Call to The House of Prayer

Appendices

Endnotes

Forward By Jorge Parrott Ph.D.

Over the last twenty years serving in missions my heart is continually wrecked by the Lord to see how many followers of Jesus in diverse cultures exhibit their unique expression displaying such faith and joy in our Lord, often in dire circumstances, unfelt by many of us in the 'cushy' West. With increasing persecution, wars, earthquakes, economic and political upheaval with shockwaves of great shaking going on globally we see end-time prophecies unfolding right before our eyes. How are we to discern the times? How are we to "know the spirits" in light of the constant news that is far stranger than fiction? We must seek God for revelation of His plans. This book presents just such an effort.

I have asked the Lord regularly to introduce me to remarkable men and women who are making a real and lasting impact for the Kingdom of God in the earth with fruit that remains. Scott Husted is one of these remarkable people, and has become a dear friend. Scott and I first met six years ago. Scott is unforgettable in his love, joy and passion for the Lord and this new creation life. We live thousands of miles apart, yet in the spiritual realm we stand very close with hearts knit together by similar revelations of the heart of the Father. Scott's is a voice that needs to be heard. Of course, the reader should take every prophetic word to the Lord.

Each time I read Scott's writings I feel a sense of urgency for souls and divine strategies to reach and disciple as many as we can, while we can. I also sense great peace and a holy hunger and curiosity to see and listen to what the Holy Spirit is speaking through Scott. He brings a refreshing perspective to the seemingly increasing confusion and darkness we see. He ties together what the Word says and Holy Spirit's breath with great clarity. With fresh revelation and a strong anointing Scott casts God's vision regarding the Ring of Fire and the end-time House of David houses of prayer strategy through worship, intercession and revelation.

As time passes the world is hearing more and more about the Pacific Ring of Fire. What an amazing tapestry of diverse tribes and cultures exist all around this immense world zone. This book echoes the emerging truth that the Lord is connecting His awakening Bride to begin to move 'as one'. Our Lord is our creator and that creative spirit sparked by the Ancient of Days ripples through the many 'ethnos' or people groups in such a confirming way of how he has written 'upon our hearts' his plan and perfect will his wondrous ways to perform. Scott is tapping into this currently emerging work of God in the earth. We read in Phil. 1:6 (TPT) "*I pray with great faith for you*, because I'm fully convinced that the One who began this glorious work in you will faithfully continue the process of maturing you and will put his finishing touches to it until the unveiling of our Lord Jesus Christ!"

What an exciting time we live in! We have the high privilege of aligning with and participating with the Lord of the Harvest in this day of the greatest response to the gospel the world has ever known. We have the exciting chance to live out the greatest adventure of faith ever dreamed of, and walking it out in the fullness of His joy! May you be illuminated, encouraged, empowered, and challenged by the light and truth and joy found in this book!

Scott opens his heart here, in an amazingly honest telling of his trials, heartaches, darkness and spiritual warfare his family and he have persevered through to see the birth of this vision begin to gain traction and bear fruit. Like Noah laboring to obey the Lord for one hundred twenty years, Scott, Dionne and Jonah have held firmly to the words and promises of the Lord even when many would ask if they heard clearly... when others would wonder where and when and how this could happen. Their focus, commitment and devotion in partnering with the Lord have cost them everything -- but they know that He is worth it all.

There are gems waiting to be discovered in this book and it is written for those genuinely hungry to see the Lord inhabit the praises and the lives of those ready to 'cross over' into their promised land with faith, if they faint not. I sense that even you might be the one this book is written for, in order for you to take the leap forward -- surrendering your life to the Lord to hear and obey (Shama in Hebrew) -- you are looking for a clear sign from the Lord to act as a cathartic impetus to go for it. This book holds pieces of God's plan and beautiful examples of how it may be implemented.

Jorge Parrott, Ph.D.
President of Eagle Missions, Sidney and Helen Correll Missionary Ministries since 1998, Founder and President of MorningStar University College of Theology (2007)
www.msutheology.org, www.eaglemissions.org.

Author's Forward to the New Edition

Some thought it a good idea for me to write a forward for this new edition. When I first wrote this book I knew it wasn't finished yet. The first edition was an attempt to get down in writing as much of the revelation about this new call that God was pouring out at the time as I could. I was on the floor in the War Room writing this, a culmination of five or so years of downloads about the house of prayer, how it should be undergirded in faith, with specific philosophy and values, and a little about how it should operate. Little did I know that this big vision would become even bigger, more awesome and amazing as we walked it out!

At the time of the release of the first edition of this work we had just begun to follow God in His call on our lives to the nations. Now, nearly 20 years after the first visions and words, we have walked out this call in eight countries -- and we have barely just begun. When we first received this vision and call we were living in Santa Rosa, California on the pastoral team of a local Vineyard Church. As we responded to the call on our lives to worship, intercession and revelation, God broke out in our church and touched the city.

Through that sovereign move of God we were invited to go to Kelowna, British Columbia Canada to help establish The War Room House of Prayer there. It was a blessed time of worship to God, intercession and revelation for Canada and the world -- much of what God was releasing there as far as what the house of prayer is and how to make it work is written down in this book.

After two very exciting years in Canada, God opened the door for us to help establish a Christian school outside Seoul in South Korea. There we built the school program, planted prayer and worship communities, and helped to establish K-1 House of Prayer in Seoul. After living, working, loving, praying and getting so much revelation for the heart of Korea over five years, it didn't seem right just to leave when our Christian school jobs came to an end. That's where section IV, Our Story, begins. It was a time of transition in the midst of great uncertainty and downright disillusionment as I wrestled with God and this enormous call on my life.

Now we are working on projects with our partners in multiple locations around the globe, speaking at churches and leadership conferences, teaching and training, working the "tentmaking" jobs that God has graciously provided, and squeezing in time for family in yet another set of far-flung destinations. We are walking out the rest of the story through our lives! At each turn God has given us vision to take next steps, but isn't it the steps from one level to the next that always seem the most impossible? From church workers to pastors; from pastors to house of prayer pioneers; from pioneers to international missionaries; from missionaries to conference speakers; from speakers to network leaders; from network leaders to… with God, there is no limit as the story unfolds. We invite you to live out the story with us!

Please pray for us, as you read this, that God will provide the continuing power, wisdom, grace and resources to blast us, yet again, into the next level of His call on our lives!

With love and blessings to all who read this,

J. Scott Husted

Introduction

This book is a response to the heart of God. It is written, first and foremost, as an explanation of what the House of Prayer is, as it has unfolded thus far. As such it is not intended as a theological treatise, but more as a statement of vision – a vision that God is casting abroad right now throughout the whole earth. I have taken great pains to make the initial explanatory sections as clear and simple as possible. I have also given these sections to people of differing denominational backgrounds, some that hadn't even heard of the House of Prayer before. I was surprised by the overwhelmingly positive responses, even from readers to whom this was heretofore a foreign concept. I extensively incorporated the feedback these people gave me to make it more understandable – hopefully to anyone.

This book has been written, secondly, as an explication of some of the various expressions of the House of Prayer. This aspect reflects expressions that exist currently, but is also visionary in scope. The various expressions discussed here represent major threads that are emerging within this new paradigm, threads that can be seen foreshadowed in the major biblical passages concerning the re-establishment of God's house "in that day", or nearing the end of history.

I must explain for the benefit of some readers, that much of the material contained here is visionary, even specifically revelatory – God showed it to me. If this is a stretch for you philosophically or theologically, just think of it in the same way that you might when you are "seeking God for direction", or what you may suppose it is like when someone responds to a "calling" on their life. Any kind of "Revelation" from God is just the same as these more commonly accepted instances of hearing from God. In saying that much of this material is revelatory I do not mean that I believe that God is revealing something that supercedes or adds to the Word of God handed down to us in the Bible. I do not believe this – in fact, I believe that personal revelation must always line up with the precepts, intention and heart of the Word – in fact this is the primary way that we can test any truth as God's communication to us. We could go on with a discussion of the important topic of hearing God, but that discussion is the subject of a whole new book. There are many good materials that will teach you how to hear God's voice – *A Short and Easy Method of Prayer* by Madame Jeanne Guyonne, and *Can You Hear Me?* By Brad Jersak are but a couple of very good examples. We must simply leave this discussion for the present with the great and wonderful assurance that God does want to speak to us and, as Jesus said: "My sheep listen to my voice; I know them, and they follow me…" (John 10:27).

I have dedicated this book to my wife, Dionne, and my son, Jonah. It is often difficult, and sometimes a real problem to have your husband or dad totally wrapped up in a project like this, and for so long. I appreciate their love, help and patience more than I can begin to say.

Thanks also to my father-in-law, Doug, who was always ready to give me a fresh, died-in-the-wool Baptist perspective. That often helped more than he may know. Thanks to Jeff and Kathi who let me soak, write and participate in the House of Prayer while writing this. Thanks to the students of the first class of the HOP Training School. Thank you, to many who read review copies and provided feedback. Thank you very much, Michael, who read and gave me probably the most extensive and most valuable feedback – as well as collaborating on the Kingdom Business chapter. Thank you, Jewell, for being such a huge support and encouragement. Thank you, Stacey for reading this and then being such an awesome promoter and supporter. Thank you, Thank you so much, Tom, who read the work and provided the amazing references throughout. I could not have done what Tom did in ten years all alone with a Bible and a concordance program. Tom is a gifted Biblical scholar and a dedicated House of Prayer pioneer. Because of Tom's work, the footnotes are often more anointed than the text. Again, first and last, Thank you Dionne for helping me to proofread the whole thing – without your great love and support, none of this wonderful journey would have been possible.

Section I
A Call to the House of Prayer

Chapter 1 The Volcanic Chain

I was lying on the couch in tremendous pain. This kidney stone was searing – I was sweating all over and my head was numb. My renal system was temporarily shut down as kidney and urethra were being ripped through with the most full-volume, all-out, full-body-emergency spasms of constant pain. I'd been to the hospital already, and there was not much that they could do short of knocking me unconscious with Demerol again.

My wife Dionne called from the computer: "There's a preacher in Oregon. This email says that a preacher named Todd Bentley is having a series of meetings up in a town called Albany, Oregon, and people are getting healed!" I could hear her through a fog of pain and Tylenol with codeine. What does she expect me to do, I wondered, pack up in the car and drive who-knows-how-far from Santa Rosa in Northern California into who-knows-where, hundreds of miles away in Oregon? In this kind of pain?

"There's a preacher…?" I ventured, grasping at words that eluded me through the haze as she came into the living room.

"We're supposed to go." She sounded quietly resolute.

"To Oregon?" The fog cleared a little as the shock of her statement pushed through. "With a kidney stone? I'm supposed to drive to Oregon?"

"I'll drive, if you need me to. We need God to come through for us – you just can't keep lying on the couch in this kind of pain. People are getting healed, and we need a miracle." The insane suggestion had me fully aware now.

"Are you kidding me? How am I supposed to ride in the car for hours in this kind of pain while we look for a town hundreds of miles away to go sit in church meetings and listen to a preacher we have never even heard of?"

"We need to hurry, we should leave tonight" was her only reply as she slipped down the hall to pack our bags.

By evening my pain had subsided somewhat and a growing conviction told me that Dionne was right, even though I could find no reason to embark on this strange trip. We loaded up, tucked our nine-year-old son Jonah into the back seat and set off for Oregon. I settled into the passenger seat, found the city of Albany on the map of Oregon in the car atlas and felt the kidney pain fading, strangely, for the first time in days. I felt good enough to drive by the time we stopped for gas outside Redding, four hours north.

It was deep night as we headed into the mountains further north around the Shasta Lakes area, with a full moon illuminating the hills and valleys as we sped through. Mists wound around the steep mountainsides as we climbed up and up the ribbon of highway. I woke Jonah up so that he wouldn't miss the spectacular moonlit views. We all looked down from our lofty position and realized that we were above the clouds, with fingers of the lake shimmering in the moonlight below them.

We were at once overcome and energized by the overpowering beauty of the mountains. As we all bubbled over in exuberant awe I began to tell Jonah about these mountains – that they are part of a chain of volcanic mountains that runs through the Northwest. We mounted up through pass after pass. As I told about Mt. Shasta and the other old volcanoes along the chain, the Spirit of the LORD began to come on me and I began to prophesy spontaneously. "God has set a sign in the earth that runs through the Northwest: a volcanic chain of mountains that are connected by an underground river of fire." The mountain ranges crowded and fell away around us as we sped through.

I went on: "God has written into the land, in its very creation, the prophetic end-time destiny of this whole region. The volcanic mountains running through the Northwest are physical signs, marking the places where God wants to establish the Mount of the Fire of the LORD in Houses of Prayer[1] from California to Canada. He is establishing this

---

[1] As seen in Isaiah 56:7, and reiterated by Jesus in Mt. 21:13, Mk. 11:17, and Lk.

spiritual volcanic chain[1] throughout the Northwest connected by an underground river of fire; and all at once, at His command they are going to blow! When they pour forth it will be an outpouring of the fire of The LORD[2], it will fill this region, sweep across the continent, and flow from there around the world."

As I was speaking this to my family I began to call out the names of the mountains that stand as part of the volcanic chain in the Northwest. "Lassen", I called out, "Mount Saint Helens…Mount Hood …Mount Rainier…" We sped up over mountains and down through mountain valleys. One of these names that I called out was "Kelowna". I looked at Dionne and said, "What's a Kelowna?"

"It must be a mountain in Canada, or something." She replied.

As I continued calling out the names of mountains we came around a long descending sweep of highway which brought us down out of the mountain ranges beyond Shasta Lake. Suddenly the massive presence of snow-clad Mount Shasta loomed before us, standing glimmering in the moonlight.

"Shasta!" I called out, stretching my hand out toward this most breathtaking of markers along God's volcanic chain.

We rolled into Albany at eight in the morning. We had driven nine hours through the night. We stopped to have breakfast and went on to find the church. There at a large old storefront that housed the Vineyard, people were gathering for a morning meeting. By noon we had worshipped, shared some teaching, had prayer for the city and brought worship out onto the front steps of the old courthouse in downtown Albany. The evening meetings were packed with eager hearts from all over the West Coast. I got powerful healing prayer for my kidney stones, but even more God was planting in me the fire of the destiny of the volcanic chain and a new direction in my life.

It was during that week at the Vineyard in Albany that we first heard about Kelowna in Todd's meetings. He spoke about the

---

19:46.

[1] Psalm 65:5,6; note that vs. 4 is referring to God bringing His chosen into His house. Also Psalm 144:5.

[2] As prophesied in Isaiah 44:3 and Joel 2:28-30.

ministries centered in Kelowna, specifically about Patricia King's influence in his life. "It's a city!" I shouted to Dionne over the loud ministry. I immediately ran out and bought a map of Oregon, Washington and southern British Columbia.

The LORD continued to encourage me to research the volcanic mountains throughout the Northwest. I gathered more maps and books, plotting out everything. On these maps I marked the volcanic mountains, making it simple to see the nearby towns and cities where the Houses of Prayer are to be established. During this research time God spoke to me that the volcanic chain is going to be a big move, bigger than I had previously thought. He then uncovered the biggest part of the message -- that the volcanic chain in the Northwest is only a small part of a much larger volcanic chain that encircles the globe -- the Ring of Fire.

As I researched further I discovered that the Ring of Fire is a volcanic chain that stretches around the whole Pacific Rim, touching a huge number of nations. I began to see that God intends for the move of God along the volcanic chain in the Northwest to cover the North American continent and then move around the Ring of Fire -- affecting all the nations that it touches[1]. God has set the Ring of Fire as a physical demarcation for a ring of passion-filled Houses of Prayer He wants to set in the earth as an engagement ring for His bride[2]. A ring of passion, power, signs and wonders in the fire of the LORD; the very Mount of the LORD established in the earth.

After a considerable amount of research God has shown much about what He intends to do in this work, as well as spotlighting many of the volcanic regions where He wants Houses of Prayer planted all over the Ring of Fire. Kelowna, British Columbia is one of those regions, one to which my family and I moved for a season in order to follow His direction to help in the establishment of the House of Prayer in the earth.

The area around Santa Rosa in Northern California and the area around Kelowna in Canada share a unique ancient heritage, and a

---

[1] As Jesus said we will do in Acts 1:8.
[2] The Bride as seen in Rev. 21:2, and vs. 9 as bride of the lamb Jesus.

connection along the Ring of Fire. It turns out that the Central Okanagan area around Kelowna is one of the largest volcanic fields in the world. The whole area is a volcanic field that can be seen in many volcanic mountains and cliffs; the cliffs being evidence of volcanic activity so widespread that at one time lava pushed up through the very cracks in the ground. We moved from Santa Rosa, California, situated on the edge of the Clearlake basin -- also one of the largest volcanic fields in the world. These two regions share a unique end-time destiny, along with other important points along this Northwestern chain of fire.

A Surprising Confirmation

Early in the morning on June 6, 2003 a friend of mine, Shelley Petracek, had a singular experience that she can only take to have been an open vision. In this vision she saw a map of the west coast of North America with a Star of David[1] superimposed upon it. The voice of the LORD spoke to her and said: "I am about to restore the Tabernacle of David[2] in this region." Shelley continues:

"I believe that the LORD will touch this entire region, but the points of the star are very significant. As the Tabernacle of David is restored, so will come the harvest of all harvests[3]!"

In December of 2003 Shelley and her husband Don invited my family for dinner. Over dinner Shelley and Don, and Dionne and I were relaxing and sharing what the LORD had been saying to each of us. Shelley began to share her vision of the Star of David. I was dumbfounded. I eagerly began to share the word of the Volcanic Chain that God had given me years before. The four of us exploded in astonishment and excitement. We pulled out globes and maps as we connected the two visions. After we mapped it all out we began to pray together over all of it, in fervent recognition that God is up to something big[4]! As we prayed we heard the LORD say that the Ring

---

[1] This is an interesting picture showing that Jesus himself will come down upon the Northwest, as can be understood from Rev. 22:16, as applied to this vision.
[2] As prophesied in Amos 9:11, and reiterated in Acts 15:16.
[3] Rev. 14:14-16.
[4] As in Isaiah 43:19.

of Fire is His engagement ring to the Bride[1], set in the earth as a ring of passionate houses of prayer. He continued that the Star of David is the diamond set in the engagement ring, the centerpiece of fire – a covenant token for His beloved reaching all around the Pacific Rim.

Further Confirmation of God's Engagement Announcement

Shelley and I were prompted to release these words together On February 13, 2004, as a valentine announcement to the Bride of Christ. The morning we sent out our combined word and vision it reached the desk of Deborah Ritz, an overseer of the prophetic department of New Life Church in Kelowna. At the very moment that Deborah received our submission she was busily transcribing the dreams of two young girls, and praying over what they might mean. Deborah was astounded over how all of these words and dreams seemed to confirm one another. The dreams of the girls were both of volcanic activity.

Deborah writes: "As a further confirmation of God's engagement announcement, two Kelowna area children have had dreams of volcanic/lava activity affecting the city of Kelowna. On January 7th, 2004, Kaitlyn Barrington, 4 years of age, had the following dream: 'We were at the church where my music lessons are and the teacher was teaching about cars. There was a basket beside us - we thought there was pop in it but it was hot lava.

Then we were at a park with just swings. We weren't playing; mom was just feeding the baby.

Then we were back at the church and it was full of hot lava. We were in it and swimming in it. Then we were dead. Then we were alive again - we were still at the church. When we got out of the church the land was full of hot lava and it was moving and everything was moving.'

On the night of Thursday, February 12th, 2004, Megan Ritz, 11 years of age had the following dream: 'Last night I had a dream that the mountain closest to the airport and the

---

[1] II Cor. 11:2

Okanagan Lake was a volcano, and that it was erupting. There was smoke everywhere and the volcano was spitting up fire. It was starting to erupt. God told me that what this means is that there is something major that is about to happen, and that it is going to effect the whole city. Also, above the volcano, there was a cloud that was in the form of an angel. The angel was looking out over the city.'

The volcano in Megan's dream was Knox Mountain at the northern end of the City of Kelowna, British Columbia. Research shows that Knox Mountain is actually an old, ancient volcano existing in remnant formation. The flow from this type of volcano is very liquid and flows for miles over surrounding land. Other research indicates a point in the natural development of the Central Okanagan region when 'ancient rivers began to flow and erode the valley, and large volcanoes, very explosive ones, filled up the valley forming Knox Mountain and Mount Boucherie'.

As we know even the rocks[1] and trees[2] can cry out and God makes his intentions known through many means[3]. Following is an excerpt from an editorial written on February 14, 2001, (3 years ago today), in 'The Capital News, the Central Okanogan's Best Read Newspaper', entitled 'City should dig deep for mountain top'. The editorial discussed a city council direction for the establishment of Knox Mountain as a Regional Park. The article reads, 'The local fundraising effort is called River Deep, Mountain High and it serves as an allegory for two well-known Kelowna features. River Deep would refer to Mission Creek, the single largest source of water flowing into Okanagan Lake. Mountain High would refer to Knox Mountain, the ancient volcano that dominates Kelowna's northern skyline.'

The 'city' churches, the church of the Northwest region

---

[1] As Jesus declared in Luke 19:39,40.
[2] The trees can "clap their hands" as in Isaiah 55:12, "sing out" as in I Chron. 16:33, and "rejoice" as in Psalm 96:12 and Isaiah 14:8.
[3] Hebrews 1:1.

and the bride should dig deep for the mountain top – deep into the ancient river of God that flows from his throne[1] and touches the heart of His bride[2] and of the nations[3]".

River Deep, Mountain High

Deborah's point is that there is a call going forth throughout the Northwest and throughout the world for the establishment of the Mountain of the LORD in Houses of Prayer that will be conduits for the fire of the LORD to flow across the land. There is so much more to this word, many more layers and many more implications for God's end-time plan. The central point upon which my word, Shelley Petracek's vision, and the little girls' dreams all agree is that the establishment of the House of Prayer – the Mount of the fire of the LORD -- along the West Coast of North America is absolutely key to God's end-time purposes in North America and in the world. These Houses of Prayer act as touch points to heaven, as doorways to accessing the substance of heaven so that we as citizens of heaven[4] can bring it down into the earth[5].

The lover says to his beloved in Song of Songs 8:5-7: "...Place me like a seal over your heart, like a seal on your arm; for love is as strong as death, its jealousy unyielding as the grave. It burns like a blazing fire, like a mighty flame. Many waters cannot quench love; rivers cannot wash it away. If one were to give all the wealth of his house for love, it would be utterly scorned." The powerful, passionate experience of intimacy with our divine beloved is the flame of fire we are talking about, and it is absolutely essential to God's end-time plan for His people and for the earth.

Zechariah 2:5, further, tells us of the time we are stepping into: "And I myself will be a wall of fire around [my house]' declares the LORD, 'and I will be its glory within". God intends to build communities of His people in the earth that will be radical in their

---

[1] As can be seen in Rev. 22:1
[2] Ez. 11:19, 20; also ch. 36:26.
[3] Rev. 22:17.
[4] Eph. 2:19; Philip. 3:20
[5] Mt. 18:18, 19.

commitment to Him[1], and to each other[2]. This kind of unity will make the Body of Christ into a beacon[3] in the gathering darkness of the kingdoms of this world[4], like never before seen in the earth[5] . It is volcanic chains of Houses of Prayer throughout regions all over the earth that will usher in this kind of passionate experience of intimacy and unity with the heart of God, and with one another. For those who have ears to hear, let him hear!

---

[1] Even to death, Gal. 2:20, 21, II Cor. 5:15.
[2] As Jesus prayed in John 17, and as set forth in I Cor. 1:10 and I Pet. 1:22 among other references.
[3] As stated in Matt. 5:14 -16.
[4] I John 5:19.
[5] As prophesied in Isaiah 60:2.

Chapter 2 A New Thing

God is doing a new thing in the earth in this day[1]. Did I say a new thing? This work of God has been foreshadowed throughout the whole of the Bible, has been experienced by His people in prophetic foretastes throughout history, and it is what we can look forward to in greater measure as the days before us unfold[2]. This work is, however, a new thing that God is establishing in the earth for the very first time on a global scale. "The latter glory of this house shall be greater than the former', says the LORD of hosts; 'and in this place will I give peace and prosperity...'" Haggai 2:9. What is this new thing? This latter glory greater than the things that have come before it will only be brought forth in the midst of His House established in the earth. This new work of God in the earth is the establishment of His House of Prayer in cities all over the globe.

God has told us throughout His word that He would do this work in the earth in these last days. In Acts 15, James quotes the prophet Amos, " 'After these things I will return, and I will rebuild the tabernacle of David which has fallen, and I will rebuild its ruins, and I will restore it, so that the rest of mankind may seek the LORD, and all the Gentiles who are called by my Name,' says the LORD who makes these things known from long ago." (Acts 15:16, 17 & 18) The work springing up today all over the world of the establishment of the House of Prayer is a direct fulfillment of this promise of God. But what is the Tabernacle of David?

David's Tabernacle

David brought the Ark of the Covenant to Mount Zion in his own city, The City of David, not back to Moses' tabernacle (1 Chron.

---

[1] Isaiah 43:18,19, especially Isaiah 42:9.
[2] II Pet. 1:19. This scripture has special relevance to the prophetic grounding and nature of this whole book.

15:1). He pitched a tent for the ark, the seat of the very presence of God, in his own backyard -- not bringing it back to its proper religious position! What is going on here? The scriptures tell us that the ark had been taken by Israel's enemies, but those enemies had nothing but trouble while they kept it. So they sent it away with fear and gifts of apology, and God led the oxen that carried it back into Israel's territory. The Ark of God languished in dishonor at Kiriath-jearim in a house in the woods, however, while Saul was king (I Samuel, chapters 5, 6 & 7).

    When David became king God moved on David's heart to bring the ark back to a place of honor (1 Chron 13:1-3). But why Zion? Zion was the highest hill in the territory of Judah, the tribe of David. David's desire to give a home to the ark in his family territory speaks of the heart of affection that David carried for God's presence. Furthermore, the meaning of the name Judah in Hebrew is "praise". David had a heart after God[1] and relationship enough with Him to know that God is more honored on the mount of praise and worship than on the mount of sacrifice[2]. So the Tabernacle of David was established on the summit of Mount Zion with the Ark of God housed in a simple tent in the sight of the whole city.

    This was an astounding new development, for no one, including priests, could approach the ark in Moses' tabernacle. Only the High Priest could stand before the ark, and only on The Day of Atonement[3]. David understood, however, that God wants to be honored among His people in worship and praise: David knew that God inhabits the praises of His people[4]. David appointed priests, singers and musicians to minister before the ark at Zion[5]. The priests at Zion led the people day and night in praise, prayer and revelation with singing, playing instruments, petitioning, prophesying, and worshipping with all their might -- in the place of symbolic animal

---

[1] Acts 13:22
[2] Heb. 13:15.
[3] Lev. 16:11; Ex. 30:10; Heb 9:7.
[4] Psalm 22:3.
[5] I Chron. 16: 4-6.

sacrifices[1]. This foreshadowed the message of the book of Hebrews in the New Testament.

David understood that God prefers the intimate sacrifice of praise above rituals[2]. Yet David did not completely replace the established practice because he knew that the blood sacrifices must continue in Moses' tabernacle in order to cover the sins of the nation[3]. This was true because Jesus had not yet made the ultimate sacrifice[4].

Distinctive Aspects

The Tabernacle of David demonstrated a divine worship, a worship "in spirit and in truth", which had several distinctive aspects:

1   Singers and singing- 1 Chr. 15:16-27, 25:1-7
2   Musicians- 1 Chr. 23:5, 25:1-7
3   Scribes to record prayers and songs of praise; this is where much of the book of Psalms was written- 1 Chr. 16:4
4   Thanksgiving- 1 Chr. 16:4, 8, 41
5   Praise- 1 Chr. 16:4, 36
6   Psalms- 1 Chr. 16:9, Ps 98:6
7   Rejoicing and joy- 1 Chr. 16:10, 25-31 unlike solemnity of Moses' tabernacle
8   Shouting- 1 Ch.r 16:4, Ps 47:1, 5, Is 12: 6
9   Dancing- 1 Chr. 15:29, 2 Sam 6:14, Ps 149
10 Lifting up hands- Ps. 134 suggests surrender, prayer, sacrifice
11 Physical expressions of worship: kneeling, bowing down, falling down, prostration- Ps. 95:6, Deut. 9:25, Num. 16:45, Rev. 19:4
12 Seeking the LORD- 1 Chr. 16:10-11
13 Spiritual sacrifices- Ps. 27:6, 1 Pet. 2:3-5, Heb. 13:15
14 Access not just for the High Priest, but the people and priests all worshipped before the presence of God- 1 Chr. 16:4, 6, 37

---

[1] I Chron. 25:1.
[2] Psalm 51:15-17; Psalm 40:6; Psalm 69:30,31; and Psalm 50:13,14.
[3] I Chron. 16:39, 40.
[4] Heb. 9:8.

15 Intercession for others, the nation, the nations of the world with petitions, with thanksgiving, with praise- 1Chr. 16:4, many examples throughout Psalms

16 Prophecy and the other gifts of the Holy Spirit- 1 Chron. 25:1, Ps. 40:3, 6, 1 Cor. 12:28.

Foundation Stones: Worship, Intercession and Revelation

Probably the most important aspect of David's tabernacle was a new focus on praise and worship. The singing and instrumental music went on day and night, "continually before The LORD"[1]. Singers were appointed specifically[2] as well as musicians[3] who played drums, cymbals, trumpets, harps and instruments of all kinds[4]. With cymbals and trumpets, it's clear that the worship was largely not quiet and contemplative[5]. This kind of worship and praise represents a key component of any pattern for the establishment of The House of Prayer in our day.

Another major aspect of the Tabernacle of David, and one that has gone largely unnoticed by many in the church, is prayer and intercession. David appointed "...Levites to minister before the ark of the LORD, to make petition, to give thanks, and to praise The LORD..." this is prayer and intercession in the form of petitions, thanks and praise, with singing and music[6]. Further, in the book of Psalms we can find actual examples of what the content of those prayers were. In the Psalms we see intercession for others going on, prayers in the midst of personal struggles, dynamic intercession for the nation, and prayer and prophecy going forth for the nations of the world[7]. These examples of prayer and intercession stand as foundation

---

[1] Specifically shown in I Chron. 16:6,37, and outlined by "worship teams" hour by hour for twenty-four hours in I Chron. 25.
[2] I Chron. 15:16,19.
[3] II Chron. 7:6; 20:13.
[4] II Chron. 5:13.
[5] This is an understatement. The King James Bible describes it as a "loud noise" in Psalm 33:3.
[6] I Chron. 16:4-6.
[7] All of this in the Psalms? There are too many examples to begin to cite. This

stones for the activity of the House of Prayer.

Another of the key aspects of the Tabernacle of David is the operation of divine revelation[1]. Once we understand that scribes recorded many of the Psalms as they were sung spontaneously in the Tabernacle of David, we can begin to see the importance of prophecy in the practice before the ark of The LORD. It becomes clear that the spirit of prophecy active in the Tabernacle of David was strong and consistent when we consider the sheer bulk of prophecy concerning the coming of Christ that we find in the Psalms[2]. "Pursue love, and desire spiritual gifts, but especially that you may prophesy" (1 Cor 14:1). Revelation from the Spirit of God in the word and in prophetic gifting[3] is an important foundational aspect for the establishment of the House of Prayer today.

The Tabernacle of David Among Us

It was prophesied that the Tabernacle of David would be restored in the earth so that "all the Gentiles" could come into His presence[4]. The apostles understood that the Old Testament prophets spoke of this work as it began in the newly birthed church[5]. Jesus began the fulfillment of this prophecy at His death when the veil in the temple, built on the pattern of Moses' tabernacle, was miraculously torn, signifying that all of His people could now come into the very presence of God[6].

The founding of the early church was the beginning of this prophesied restoration of David's tabernacle, but this work of God has not come to fruition to the point that all the peoples of the world have an opportunity to participate in seeking the LORD. One of the major features of the Tabernacle that David set up was worship, intercession

---

should whet your appetite to search out the Psalms for yourself as in Acts 17:11.
[1] As so eloquently prayed for you in Eph. 1:17-19.
[2] "For the testimony of Jesus is the spirit of prophecy" Rev. 19:10.
[3] This is described in many places throughout the Old Testament prophets, as well as in the gospels in John 16:13, and through the exhortation of Paul in I Cor. 14:4-6.
[4] Amos 9:11.
[5] Acts 15:15-17.
[6] As described in Matt. 27:51, Luke 23:45, Heb. 10: 19-23, and Rev. 21:3.

and revelation that went on twenty-four hours a day. In our current western Christian setting the unsaved generally have only one chance per week to be exposed to the life-changing effects of God's presence in corporate worship, prayer and revelation. In most churches this amounts to a one to two hour window throughout the week. Even if you include services Sunday and Wednesday nights, the total opportunity for the unsaved to be touched by the work of heaven is slim indeed. There does not exist an established forum in our culture for ongoing worship, intercession and revelation where anyone can go and experience the life-changing effects of the presence of God among His people at any time.

The foundational truth behind the need for the establishment of the House of Prayer is that God is worthy of so much more than we give in our current western practice. This is the truth behind our worship in spirit and in truth – He is worthy[1], and He alone is worthy[2]. I could stop right here, as this supreme reason is reason enough for me to spend the rest of my days simply worshipping Him. Yet God's heart goes further. He has a desire that everyone might be saved[3]. The unsaved nations need more opportunity than we currently give to be touched by the power of heaven established on earth. This scriptural parameter, that the nations of the world will be given opportunity to know him, is important to the ultimate identification and purpose of the House of Prayer, as it links the establishment of the House of Prayer in the earth with the great harvest of souls promised at the end of the age.

We are living in the day where this Davidic worship in spirit and truth is being re-established among us. God is empowering our worship in songs and music. He is re-establishing revelation in powerful teaching and prophecy. He is igniting prayer and intercession like never before. He is also moving on the hearts of people all over the globe to establish centers where His people can gather from every group, nationality, and denomination from all over a city at any time of the day or night to worship Him. Established Houses of Prayer

---

[1] ...of all our time, all our money, of all our efforts, Rev. 4:11.
[2] Isaiah 42:8.
[3] I Tim. 2:4.

include: The War Room in Kelowna, British Columbia, The International Houses of Prayer in Kansas City, Vertical Call in Santa Rosa, California, the House of The King in Toronto, Boiler Rooms across Britain, and Prayer Network in Boston. Others that I have had some connection with include start-ups in Germany, Zambia, Turkey, Holland, Jerusalem, Fiji and Thailand.

The work of the establishment of the House of Prayer springing up today all over the world is a direct fulfillment of the promise of God to re-establish the work and heart of David's tabernacle.

Old Testament Prophets

Old Testament prophets told about this work of establishment in our day, clearly and often. One example we've just considered is the passage in Amos, quoted by James in the book of Acts, yet there are many more. Jeremiah speaks of this work in Jeremiah 31:6, "There will be a day when watchmen cry out on the hills of Ephriam, 'Come, let us go up to Zion, to the LORD our God' ". Jeremiah continues in verse 12: "They will come and shout for joy on the heights of Zion; they will rejoice in the bounty of The LORD –the grain, the new wine, and the oil..." On one level, this is a prophecy of the returning of Israel to its own land, and so pinpoints the very time in history in which we now live. Yet it is also a prophecy of the re-establishment of the presence of "The LORD our God" on "the heights of Zion". Mount Zion, of course, is the place where David's tabernacle stood, and in this statement Jeremiah is seeing a future day in which this Zion will be re-established. This Zion is the re-establishment of the House of the LORD in this day: the establishment of Davidic worship and prayer in centers dedicated to this purpose.

The well-known prophecy of the dry bones in Ezekiel 37 is another Old Testament prophecy that features God's intent for the House of Prayer. This passage is a birds-eye view of the work of God going on in the earth today. It also is a very telling prophecy of the re-establishment of the very dwelling place of God in the earth, the House of Prayer.

The bringing together of Ezekiel's dry bones is explained in the text as a re-assembling of the scattered people of Israel in their land. This physical gathering in physical Israel is going on right now. There is also a spiritual assembling going on today, of the people of God from all nations, tribes, denominations and groups into a spiritual dwelling place, the House of Prayer being established in the earth[1]. This fact is brought home clearly at the end of chapter 37: "My dwelling place will be with them; I will be their God, and they will be my people. Then the nations will know that I the LORD make Israel holy, when my sanctuary is among them forever". What is this "dwelling place", but a clear reference to the establishment of the House of Prayer? This passage also contains a link to the text in Amos, which proclaims the re-establishment of the Tabernacle of David, in its statement that through this place the nations will come to knowledge of The LORD.

One of the most potent of the Old Testament prophecies concerning the establishment of The House of Prayer in this day can be found in Isaiah 56:6, 7:

> "And foreigners who bind themselves to the LORD to serve Him, to love the name of the LORD, and to worship Him -- all who keep the Sabbath without desecrating it and who hold fast to My covenant -- these I will bring to My holy mountain and give them joy in My House of Prayer. Their burnt offerings and sacrifices will be accepted on My altar; for My house will be called a House of Prayer for all nations."

We are these foreigners! This promise is for us! It is exciting in that, as we love and worship the LORD, binding our hearts to Him, He promises to bring us to His holy mountain and establish His House of Prayer among us. God is re-establishing His physical holy mountain as He re-establishes Israel as a nation[2]. But, as we have seen portrayed in this and other passages, He is doing something new by establishing a spiritual people who are not necessarily physical Israelis[3]. He is

---

[1] He is making known to us a mystery as in Eph. 1:9, 10.
[2] A work that has been going on since 1948.
[3] As in Rom. 2:28, 29; Gal. 6:16, and other passages. I would like to stress that this is not by way of replacement of the historic ethnic Jews, but by grafting we Gentiles into the family of God as the Bible teaches in Rom. 11:24.

bringing us up, we who are "foreigners who bind themselves to the LORD", to His holy mountain and establishing among us His House of Prayer! But what, you may ask, is this spiritual holy mountain He is bringing us to? It is the very work of heaven.

The Work of Heaven

The true spiritual mountain of the LORD is, of course, the place of His throne as He rules from the highest heaven[1]. The pattern God gave to Moses for the building of the tabernacle in the wilderness was a pattern of heaven. The laver full of water pictured the glassy sea set in front of God's throne. The altar of incense spoke of the four living beings whose worship goes up before God's throne day and night, and the mercy seat reflected the very throne of God. We see this pattern of heaven in action throughout the Bible, with one of the most descriptive passages found in the book of Revelation.

In Revelation chapters 4 and 5, we see the work of heaven going on before our eyes. One day as I read through this passage, God began to ask me if I could see what was going on in this picture. "There's definitely worship going on with the elders, and the living beings, and the 'Holy, Holy, Holy' ", I replied.

"What else?" God's heart was insistent.

I looked deeper and began to realize that the Lamb came forward to open the scroll because there was no one else to do it. A verse from Romans 8 echoed through my mind: "...It is Christ that died, yea rather, that is risen again, who is even at the right hand of God, who also maketh intercession for us"[2].

"Of course", I thought, "intercession is also going on at Your throne"[3].

"Yes. Worship and Intercession... and there is one more specific activity. Can you see it?" I puzzled over the question. The worship going on in the passage is overwhelmingly clear. The intercession is there, though you have to understand it to recognize it.

---

[1] As seen in Isaiah 66:1, Psalm 103:19 and others.
[2] Rom 8:34.
[3] Heb. 7:25.

Of course The LORD gave me some help by popping the scripture from Romans into my mind. But what else was going on here? The falling down? No, that would have to be a part of the worship... Lightning, rumbling, peals of thunder... lampstands blazing... John weeping... nothing seemed like a separate specific activity. God interjected into my dwindling train of thought: "It might be difficult for you to see, because you are seeing the scene through the eyes of the observer..." God gave away the answer again.

"It's the observer! There is observation going on in heaven!" I felt triumphant, as if I had figured it out, despite God's gentle leading statements.

"You're right! And it is the job of this observer to bring the revelation he receives in heavenly places back into the earth to share with the rest of my people there". I realized that this is quite simply what John had done with his vision, and the essential activity of the observer communicating what is revealed is the reason that I could have this detailed glimpse of heaven and its operation called the book of Revelation! God continued: "This is the work of heaven --worship, intercession and revelation. And now you are privileged to enter into the very work of heaven in the House of Prayer".

This was an overwhelming revelation to me, full of explosive realizations. It was a revelation of the huge, all-encompassing role of constant, never-ending worship in heaven and in the House of Prayer -- and only because He is worthy of it. It was a revelation of the preciousness, the high calling, the intimate privilege of laying our lives down like Jesus before the throne of God in intercession[1]. It was also a revelation of the essential role of revelation in the ongoing process[2] of planting and cultivating this work of God in the earth.

The establishment of the House of Prayer is truly God's Kingdom come in the earth as it is in heaven in worship, in intercession and in revelation. These three heavenly functions going on continually before the presence of God is the very DNA of heaven, forming a three-strand cord that is to be brought into the earth and

---

[1] The need for a constant commitment to prayer can be seen in I Thess. 5:16-25, Acts 12:5-7, and Rom. 1:9, 10 among other scriptures.
[2] II Pet. 3:18; Eph. 1:16-18.

planted as the DNA of the House of Prayer. Bringing this work of heaven into the earth is our great and high privilege right now, unprecedented in human history.

Section II

The Foundations of the House of Prayer in Structure, in Function and in Content

Section 1

The Foundations of the Theory of Migration Systems in Function and Content

Ch 3 The Three-Strand Cord: God's DNA for the House of Prayer

God's Foundational Structure
  The foundational structure that the LORD has revealed for the establishment of the House of Prayer is the structure of the Three-Strand Cord: Worship, Intercession, and Revelation. These functions are the work of heaven in the earth; the work of the priesthood. This structure is the veritable DNA at the core of everything that is part of the House of Prayer.
  This three-strand structure has implications at every level of the structure, practice and content of the House of Prayer. It requires thinking about structuring life, ministry and leadership always in terms of teams that carry these three functions.
  These three functions, taken together, are the work of heaven. The throne room scenes in the book of Revelation show us a picture of the very work that is going on in heaven. Here we can observe worship and intercession going on constantly before the throne, and revelation going on as well, as can be seen in the role of John, the observer and writer of the account.
  A look into the Old Testament shows that these three functions are the core of the duties of priests in the Holy Place. A picture of the function of worship can be seen in the altar of incense, filling the Holy Place with a sweet aroma. The function of intercession can be seen portrayed in the table of showbread, the table of the bread of fellowship. The function of revelation can be seen pictured in the seven-branched lampstand, illuminating all that goes on in the Holy Place in its light.
  The three-strand work of heaven is shown throughout all of the duties of priests. Priests assist in the unloading of burdens for the

purpose of sacrifice, direct the people to the place of His presence, and light the way into the secret place, where we all can minister before the great and awesome heart of our God. We in this day have the unprecedented opportunity, only hinted at through history, to enter into the work of heaven and establish it in our own cities. We are being called now to enter our calling as a nation of kings and priests, ministering the three-strand DNA of worship, intercession and revelation before the throne of God day and night. This is what the House of Prayer movement is all about.

The Three-Strand Cord:
How the elements of the three-strand cord, the DNA of the House of Prayer, reflect corresponding elements of Heaven seen in Revelation chapter 4 and the Exodus Tabernacle.

H.O.P.	Revelation	Tabernacle
Worship	Creatures Rev. 4:6	Altar of Incense Ex. 30:1
Revelation	7 Lamps Rev. 4:5	Lampstand Ex. 25:31
Intercession	24 Elders Rev. 4:4	Table of Fellowship Ex. 25:23

The strand of worship is the foundation of the House of Prayer. The priestly function of worship leads out in every effort. It is the function that opens doors; in the hearts of people, in heavenly realms and within the heart of God. In worship we pour out the burning incense of our Love for God over Him as a pleasing fragrance, and it is that Love -- from Him, to Him, and to each other -- that must be the foundation of everything else that we do. Without Love we are nothing. The worship function is the leader through the veils of this world, through the veil of the flesh, through our own personal veils, and into the presence of God; right into His arms. Worship is founded in, and comes from the heart of the Holy Spirit our great guide, who leads us on the path into the presence of Jesus.

The strand of intercession is the next step, our hearts' cry as we come into His presence. It is the declaration of our love, and our response to what we begin to see and experience as we come in through the veil, into an experience of His heart as priests. Intercession is our response to God's heart; our breaking and partaking of the bread of His love, but also our entering into that brokenness with Him in repentance as we see our own darkness mirrored in the radiant truth of His Love. It is also our priestly outcry against the darkness and injustice that surrounds us in this world. The place of intercession is the table of our communion with Him, in His death and into the power of His resurrection. The function of intercession is founded in, and comes from the heart of Jesus; the one who stands night and day making intercession for us before the throne of the Father.

The strand of revelation is the function of covering and uncovering, moving us deeper into the many courts of intimacy with the heart and mind of God. It is the priestly role of covering for the protection of the team, covering the ministry going forth and the recipients of that ministry for safety; being alert to the needs and foibles of all involved, and being willing to meet all with a heart of caring, Love and help. It is the priestly role of lifting up the light of His wisdom, burning in the seven Spirits of God before His throne; uncovering the Glory of God for revelatory instruction, direction and the power to live out of this place of intimacy and revelation. Revelation is founded in, and comes from the heart of the Father who loves us with an unfathomable love, and wants to reveal Himself to us.

All three functions are prophetic functions, teaching and revelatory functions requiring team members that are coming into some level of proficiency in their gifting. What we are speaking of is ultimately prophetic worship, prophetic intercession and prophetic revelation. All three are quite definitely leadership functions -- priestly functions -- and require a minimum level of maturity to lead. In fact, God is instituting the Three-Strand Cord model as a new model for leadership. The terms worship leader, intercession leader, and revelation leader are completely appropriate, and begin to re-focus our concept of leadership as a team function: more as servants and door openers to the whole body or group involved. These are not to function as the sole "official performers" of their functions, but as leaders and facilitators into their areas that will rely on the movement of the Holy Spirit. These team leaders act as servants, opening the doors that God indicates for the rest of those present to come through, in order that all may participate corporately in the priestly work of heaven before the throne.

Of course all of the team members may be gifted in many areas, and all will bring some of each function as they minister together, whether in general leadership roles within the House of Prayer, or in leading specific sessions. However, it is important that there are always members of every team that consciously take responsibility for a particular Three-Strand function, and that the functions are all respected and facilitated. This will require that the functions be acknowledged within the team, whatever the team's task, and that certain team members take responsibility for a function to see that each operates fully, according to the leadership of the Holy Spirit.

Implications of the Three-Strand-Cord

The structure of the Three-Strand-Cord as the basis of the function of the House of Prayer illustrates many things about God's blueprint for the functioning of the House of Prayer. It shows that as priests we need each other – we need every part -- to function as the House of Prayer, the work of the very throne room of God established in the earth. It shows that God's pattern, ultimately God's sovereign rule, must be at the center of the structure and operation of the House of Prayer. It shows that this new structure must be completely relational: in the secret place with God first and then among one another. The blueprint of God's throne room shows that the structure and operation of the House of Prayer cannot be based on the leadership of a man or a group of men. This new structure is based completely on the mind, plan and direction of God grounded in abandoned intimacy with Him in order to receive our instructions, and radical love and faith in order to walk those instructions out.

The Priestly model requires thinking about structuring life, ministry and leadership always in terms of teams that carry these three functions. In forming worship teams it is important that we have separate members that can minister as worship leader, as intercessory leader, and as prophetic elder. In forming ministry teams we must have a member who keeps in mind the magnification of our God, one who looks for the word of Spirit, and one who covers and uncovers; covering the team and the ministry going forth for safety, and uncovering the rhema word of God to reveal His glory and power.

Teams operate more like an organism than an institution. The necessity of organism as the model for team building in the House of Prayer is that the three-strand cord of worship, intercession and revelation are spiritual functions rather than practical tasks. This has many implications, an important one being there must be a level of relationship within the team in order for the team to work together effectively. With simple practical tasks it is possible to put nearly any willing individuals together and get a job done. Three-strand teams, however, must have a relational foundation. A foundation of relationship offers the strength to support a new level of openness, vulnerability and honest communication – a level that necessary to the depth of the task, and is not achieved in organizational structures. As an organism the three-strand teams need time to develop heart communication, trust and skill to weave the several functions together.

Its three-strand DNA means that the House of Prayer must operate on a values base rather than a base of regulations. Every House of Prayer must develop a set of relational values, and core values of belief that everyone must subscribe to if they are going to be able to take up this depth of sacred service together. In beginning a local House of Prayer it is crucial that the whole group hammer out a set of relational values that include a commitment to honesty, communication, integrity, and more. This set of values should be brief, clear, practical, and everyone must be able to sign on the dotted line in a personal commitment to live these relational values out. It is at this point that the real challenge begins, as we make efforts to live out the values we have committed to.

These values must be respected, and we must go to the point of challenging one another on the basis of the values when problems or questions arise. At the same time, the outworking of these values cannot be inviolate; the team must be constantly in the process of re-evaluating and sharpening their practice of the community values for these to operate as a vibrant foundation for brotherly love within the community.

One important aspect of the priestly team base is families. God has always called families. The priesthood in the tabernacle was based on families. It was a family who baked the bread of the Presence every morning. It was a family that pressed the olives for oil and tended the flames of the lampstand. It was a family that formulated the oils and incense for exclusive use before the presence of God. It was families working together, and each family pulling together with the other teams that fulfilled all of the myriad functions of the priestly service. This shows that the calling of priesthood runs in families and priestly mantles are meant to be passed down from generation to generation. The foundational structure that the LORD has revealed for the establishment of the House of Prayer is the structure of the Three-Strand Cord: Worship, Intercession, and Revelation. The Three-Strand Cord structure is a structure of priestly functions. The establishment of the three-strand cord structure as the core structure of every aspect of the House of Prayer is a work of establishing the functions of the altar of incense, the table of the bread of fellowship, and the seven-branched lampstand in the earth: establishing the works of the Holy Place into the earth as it is in heaven.

The work of priests is a work of teams; the priesthood has always operated on the basis of teams working together. The priesthood pattern that God has given us for the foundation of the House of Prayer is extremely relational; based on intimacy and faith among all of us, and between us and God, with the direction of The Holy Spirit as the head. This priestly structure is the veritable DNA at the core of everything in the House of Prayer.

Conclusion

Worship, intercession and revelation is the very work of heaven, and forms a three-strand cord that is the foundation for bringing the work of heaven into the earth. As Ecclesiastes 4:12 states: "And if one prevail against him, two shall withstand him; and a three-strand cord is not quickly broken". So we see that worship by itself can prevail against the enemy of our souls, but worship and intercession together will give the strength to withstand that enemy. When we bring all three together, however, combining worship, intercession and revelation we have a three-strand cord that will make it possible to push back the darkness and plant the Kingdom of God in the earth. Every aspect of The House of Prayer, then, is established, organized and operates on a concept of the three-strand cord of worship, intercession and revelation. As history progresses we will need the divine strength of the three-strand cord.

The concept of the three-strand cord can be seen reflected in the organization and leadership for the House of Prayer. The functions of worship, intercession and revelation in the operation of the House of Prayer parallel the roles of the priest, the king and the prophet in the organization and leadership of the House of Prayer.

The element of worship can be seen in the *priestly* role of the House of Prayer.

The element of intercession corresponds to the *kingly* role of the House of Prayer.

The element of revelation comes forth in the *prophetic* role of the House of Prayer.

God's power flowing through these strands in the structure and operation of The House of Prayer will bring support to, and renew the strength of participating churches in the area, it will restore the homes that it touches and it will ultimately spark transformation of the city.

Ch 4 God's Pattern for the Function of the House of Prayer: The Pattern of Heaven

Functions of the Pattern of Heaven

     Years ago, during a beautiful time of worship, the LORD gave me a vision that illuminates God's pattern of heaven as He has ordained it in the earth, a blueprint for the operation of the House of Prayer. This blueprint is seen in the functions of the tabernacle; the plan of heaven established in the earth. This is the plan that God has always given for the establishment of His house in the earth.
I was sitting in the sanctuary of our simple church building, set in the midst of a small light industrial complex. We all sang from our hearts, and a sweet, profound weight of the presence of God settled in on us. As I gazed at the cross that stood on the stage in front, suddenly the roof of the building disappeared and a bright light flooded in. The cross was tall, magnificent as a throne and radiant as the sun, with a river of water flowing from its base, through the building, and out the front door. The musicians were dressed in white robes, and sung while holding up bowls of incense at the foot of the cross. I was one of these, singing and worshipping at the foot of the cross.
     Soon I became tired and couldn't lift my bowl of incense quite so high. At that point someone came and offered to take my bowl. I gratefully gave it to them, relieved to take a rest. I was directed to a row of small chairs that were spaced regularly along the wall. Happily, I sat down in one.
     To my utter surprise, no sooner had I sat down than the chair swiftly lifted high into the air. It stopped breathlessly at the top of the wall. I was suddenly overcome by a beautiful panoramic view. I could see out over the hills and valleys of the surrounding area. I saw tree-

topped hillsides, roads crowded with travelers, and the river flowing out from the sanctuary into the countryside. Inside the sanctuary I could see that there were a handful of people dressed in white like me, serving bread and wine at a table on one side of the river. More were standing in a group on the other side proclaiming the magnificence of God in beautiful counterpoint to the music and singing. Down at the entrance some were coming in and going out, helping people through the doorway and helping them take off heavy packs and bags. Others were helping people down to the water's edge, where, up to their waists, there were little groups in white singing in the river and helping to wash and heal those that had come in.

    Outside, over the wall, I saw groups engaged in skirmishes as if at war, clouds of dust in the distance telling of approaching forces, and small groups of wounded scattered here and there. I started to call down what I saw to those inside the walls. Those at the entrance who were going out to find and to rescue heard what I called out, and knew where to go to find those who were wounded. The groups who were helping and serving others heard and knew what to prepare for, and those ministering to God heard and knew the needs and thanks to lift up. As I called down, I began to notice others that were dispersed around the top of the wall also calling down from their high seats.

    After a short while up in my seat on the wall, I felt refreshed and invigorated, and eager to return to my place at the foot of the cross. At this point the chair swept back down to the floor under its own power. I returned to my place with my bowl of incense at the foot of the cross and I looked down the river taking in the beauty of the whole thing working together. Those singing, lifting their bowls before the cross, those proclaiming, lifting up the light, those breaking bread with the hungry, those seeking the wounded and lost, those washing the hurting in the river, those watching on the wall, all living and breathing life in their places with joy toward one goal -- the work of heaven. All these functions working together in concert at the foot of the cross as a single beautiful unit: the House of God in the earth[1].

---

[1] See Eph. 2:21, 22 for a beautiful prophetic description of the building of this "holy temple", this "dwelling of God" among the Christians in Ephesus.

This extensive vision lays open the functional pattern of heaven as God has desired to plant it in the earth. This is the pattern for the government and operation of the Kingdom that God has desired for His people throughout the ages: a kingdom of priests, each operating in his own area of gifting, in relationship to the rest of the body, with God Himself as the head. This vision shows that the varied functions of the House of Prayer, however distinct, must operate together as a whole, as a team of teams. The pattern of the priesthood God has set in place as the pattern of heaven in the earth shows us clearly that the plan, purpose or efforts of any person or group cannot accomplish the establishment and operation of the House of Prayer. For it to be effective in a region, the House of Prayer must be an effort of the body as a whole. The House of Prayer may only be established in the earth by implementing the pattern that God has established for the place of His throne, and by the orchestration of the Spirit of God, as a team of teams, an effort of a kingdom of priests.

The Pattern of Heaven:
How the elements of the House of Prayer correspond to the elements of Heaven seen in Revelation chapter 4 and the elements of the Exodus Tabernacle.

H.O.P.	Revelation		Tabernacle	
YHVH	Throne	Rev. 4:2	Mercy Seat	Ex. 25:10
Worship	4 Creatures	Rev. 4:6	Altar of Incense	Ex. 30:1
Revelation	7 Lamps	Rev. 4:5	Lamp stand	Ex. 25:31
Intercession	24 Elders	Rev. 4:4	Table of Fellowship	Ex. 25:23
Instruction	Crystal Sea	Rev. 4:6	Laver	Ex. 30:17
Mercy & Justice	Door	Rev. 4:1	Altar of Sacrifice	Ex. 27:1

The priestly pattern of the function of the House of Prayer further reinforces the foundational necessity of vertical and horizontal relationship as the basis for the structure and function of the

House of Prayer. This is the pattern of the cross: laying everything of ourselves down[1] to make intimate, personal relationship with Christ the absolute first necessity in our lives[2], and relationship with each other in a team structure the second[3].

The pattern of heaven operating in the context of priestly teams sheds further light on the relational, organismic design[4] God has always had in mind for the establishment of His kingdom in the earth. Within an organism each cell contains the DNA instructions for the whole being. In just such a way, each believer has the written word[5] as well as the whole Holy Spirit living inside[6]. With this kind of design our hand does not need a hierarchy of leaders to guide it[7] – the head leads and guides[8] the hand as each part works together. This is the design and purpose of God for His kingdom of priests bringing the work of heaven into the earth.

Further, the organismic, relational pattern that God has given us in the three-strand team operates in many practical ways that make controlling hierarchy unnecessary[9]. This is not to say that there is no leadership within the House of Prayer; on the contrary, leadership in the context of teams takes its proper place in roles of mentorship, caring, facilitation and servanthood[10]. Traditional hierarchy becomes unnecessary, firstly, as we are all working together, striving for love, listening to the directions of the Holy Spirit, moving together as one. Next, if we are operating in our area of gifting we will begin to move rather spontaneously. As we work in a cooperative manner, helping

---

[1] II Cor. 5:13-15 that we "should no longer live for ourselves".
[2] As in Mark 12:30, "Love the Lord our God…"
[3] As in Mark 12:31, "…and Love our neighbor…"
[4] Eph. 4:16 so beautifully portrays God's organismic design for His Kingdom.
[5] We live the word as well as have the written word: II Cor. 3:2, 3.
[6] The *Whole* Holy Spirit as in Rom. 8:9; not, as some may believe, a "part" of the Holy Spirit.
[7] "…One God who is over *ALL*…" Eph. 4:6.
[8] Col. 2:19
[9] Just as the domineering, ambitious, controlling Diotrephes was reproved in III John 9&10.
[10] Caring rather than ruling over as seen in Heb. 13:17, and Acts 20:28, those who "keep watch", "guarding", "overseeing", "shepherding".

one another[1] , we will have less and less need for specific supervisory intervention. As we gain experience in our gifting and in working within a team, the need for immediate supervision diminishes further[2] . As the team begins to develop cohesiveness, the relationships within the team become nurturing toward learning and growth, and toward needed support and positive motivation. As we walk with one another in committed relationship, the availability of good feedback from our teammates grows, and the relevance of authoritarian reviews diminishes[3] . In these ways and many more, control by hierarchical superiors in the House of Prayer becomes redundant as leadership, motivation and nurture arises from the teams themselves, a kingdom of priests submitted to one another under Christ our head.

The Priestly functions in the context of the Three-Strand-Cord

The priestly role of ministering in worship before God and His people is necessary and primary. In worship He gently begins to take our burdens. In worship we come before Him to offer our lives as a living sacrifice[4], and in worship we step up to His cleansing presence where we can be washed of every stain[5].

The practice of worship, then, gives rise to the cry of our hearts in intercession and proclamation, like the ancient priests praying for God's people and proclaiming His goodness. This dynamic give-and take between worship and intercession weaves a spiritual dialog -- a platform for intimacy with Him and one another, a true communion of His heart with ours in deep fellowship.

If all we had were this profound and joyous communion in the very presence of God[6], it would be enough. However, the heart of God once stirred in this manner is moved toward mercy and justice for the world around us. If our hearts are moving deeply into His, then our

---

[1] Rom. 12:10, Eph. 5:21, serving, honoring, giving preference, submitting to one another.
[2] Eph. 4:15, this is part of "growing up"!
[3] Again, Eph. 4:15, & Col. 3:16, "teaching and admonishing one another".
[4] Rom. 12:1
[5] Is. 1:17&18
[6] II Cor. 13:14

hearts will be moved also. This means that the more of God's heart we partake of, the more of His heart for the world we will begin to carry[1]. In the priestly work of intercession we bring the burdens of the world, and place them on the fire of His altar. In intercession we can dip the wounds of the world into His healing flood. This will move us to reach out to people in the world around us with the bread of His presence, like the priests of old, bringing bread to His table daily. In intercession we come into the bread of the fellowship of His suffering and His joy, and we come into the light of His word for a broken world.

As the incense of our worship and intercession goes up before His presence, He releases the lightning from His throne: He answers with power. Once we have entered into the heart of God in worship and intercession God responds. It is an overwhelming aspect of His great heart: He responds to us. God is the God Who Is, and who desires to be known. This is the priestly service of revelation from the word, and from the Spirit.

This place of divine revelation is deeper than the mind of man. It is deeper and more powerful than our own thoughts or expressions[2]. Most of the people of God have experienced this at one time or another, the times this kind of deep revelation fairly leaps out from the pages of the word[3], especially when we've been in a place of worship or profound prayer. This kind of "rhema" revelation is what we're talking about here, whether it comes to us through the reading of the word[4], through a direct answer in prayer, or through visions and dreams. Any time God speaks to us the power comes from out of His throne to accomplish His word. This rhema revelation from the heart of God is the light of the priestly work in the Holy Place, a light as though from the seven-branched lampstand in the presence of God.

As all of the priestly functions come forth in the context of worship, intercession and revelation they begin to form a flow of the love of God for the world. This flow will begin to attract people from

---

[1] II Cor. 5:18, 19&20
[2] Dan 2:22, I Cor. 2:7-11
[3] These are experiences where "…the eyes of our understanding are enlightened…" Eph. 1:18.
[4] Ps. 119:130

the body and from the world, from all walks of life. As numbers increase the need arises for a community of people walking in the depths of intimacy with God who can function in the many priestly areas. Seeking the lost, calling them in, unpacking their burdens that they may come through the door, as at the altar of sacrifice, leading them into the river of God's Love and walking with them through the healing they may need, all become essential functions of God's house. Then calling them into the light of His word and the table of fellowship[1], ultimately to stand before His throne with their own bowl of incense, all of these become important functions of the House of Prayer and God's order of growth, equipping and release[2].

We as a people can only do any of this through the working of the Holy Spirit through us and the gifts He has given us – none of it can be about implementing a program or format of human design. We do, however, have the blueprint of a spiritual design for the House of Prayer in the cycle of priestly service. It is important to note that all of the functions of the pattern of heaven must be in place, and functional. That means that we need priests equipped and ready for service in all areas. We need the worship, the healing, the mentoring and teaching – in fact, the full five-fold ministry[3], or six-fold with the five directed by the One -- all available and in operation for the House of God to function in the blueprint that God has given. God calls us a kingdom of priests. It is His design that we should structure and operate under His pattern of priestly service, with Jesus Himself as our King and High Priest.

---

[1] I Jn. 1:3
[2] Eph. 4:12,13 "…attaining… to the mature Man… the fullness of Christ".
[3] As listed in Eph. 4:11.

The Pattern of the New Man:

The functions of the five-fold ministry, as seen in Eph. 4:11, operating under Christ our Head, correspond to the functional elements of the Pattern of Heaven.

	H.O.P.	Revelation	Tabernacle
Jesus Alpha	YHVH	Throne	Mercy Seat
Apostles	Worship	Creatures	Altar of Incense
Prophets	Revelation	7 Lamps	Lampstand
Pastors	Intercession	24 Elders	Table of Fellowship
Teachers	Instruction	Crystal Sea	Laver
Evangelists	Mercy & Justice	Altar	Altar of Sacrifice
Jesus Omega	Invitation	Door	The Way

"…Until we all attain the unity of the faith, and of the knowledge of the Son of God, to a mature man, to the measure of the stature of the fullness of Christ" Eph. 4:13.

CH 5 Content of the House of Prayer: A Journey to the Tree of Life

Clearer Vision

Early on Dionne and I often discussed the scripture, words and visions that we were grappling with, attempting to define more clearly the vision that God had been giving us, reaching for a clearer view of the House of Prayer that God is bringing us into. At the same time we were trying to delineate characteristics of the kind of content that would promote the kind of community that we see God building.

Suddenly, one time as I was trying to articulate something of this new way of living among one another, I began to see myself standing in a pile of debris. It was faint at first, but as I focused on what was around me in the vision and started to tell Dionne what I was seeing, it came clearly into view. I was in a huge pile of leaves and twigs, and I was trying to eat from them. They were hard and sharp, with twigs poking me and sticks impeding my movement. I started to realize that this was a picture of the church the way it has been. It seemed that it had once been a tree, but was now divided and disjointed as though it had gone through a chipper/shredder. There was very little root in the pile, some chipped up wood that must have been a trunk, but the pile was made up mostly of cut up branches, twigs and leaves. I could find no fruit.

As I searched through the pile for any sustenance, my attention was drawn upward and outward before me. When I looked up I saw a tree. A whole tree. A large and beautiful tree that stretched fully in my view from topmost branches to root tips. It was large and imposing and radiating light. I waded out of the refuse pile toward this shining vision whose extensive roots, massive trunk, and dense canopy of fruit, leaves and branches beckoned to me to come and enjoy. I saw that the fruit was good for eating, and the leaves were good for healing. I realized that this must be the Tree of life[1], and the other tree must have been the Tree of the Knowledge of Good and Evil[2]. For so long the church has majored on right and wrong, rules and regulations, our own human goodness or depravity; and has maintained control by strength of religion.

As I looked I saw that the Tree of Life is all about the story of what God has done, is doing, and will do for His people. The roots are the story of what God has done in history. The trunk is the story of what He is doing and has done in our individual lives, and the branches are the story of what God will do in blessing, healing, providing for, and establishing His kingdom among His people.

The True Foundation of Faith and Practice

We are in the time of the restoration of all things[3]! God is re-establishing the fallen tent of David, and in that He is calling His people to the faith and practice that He has intended from the foundation of the world. This is a faith and practice that will take its place as the content of the worship, intercession and revelation that is the substance of the House of Prayer, but even more, it is a faith and practice that will usher in the establishment of the Kingdom of God in the earth, as "…the kingdoms of this world are become the Kingdom of our LORD, and of His Christ; and He shall reign forever and ever!" Rev. 11:15.

---

[1] Gen. 2:9, Rev. 22:2 – The River is beginning to flow. The trees are being planted..
[2] Gen. 2:9.
[3] Acts 3:21.

Traditionally we as a church have often been starving instead of moving in faith and power, because our theology and subsequent actions have been based in a theology of man's fall, in the tree of the knowledge of good and evil. This is why the church has been so concerned with sin management, so concerned with programs and so overly concerned that God and man take note of our every righteous deed[1]. We have built the church on the power of the knowledge of good and evil instead of the power of the knowledge of the grace of God, the true ways of God, that Jesus died to bring us.

In this day, however, God is calling us to found our theologies and resulting actions in His work of grace on the cross, the establishment of the Kingdom embodied in the Tree of Life. For indeed, the Cross of Christ is the Tree of Life. The cross is founded in God's plan of redemption from before the foundations of the world[2]; it stands today in the stories of our own personal redemption from sin and death; and it branches out to the world bearing the power of the blood of Christ, given for the healing of the nations. The form of the cross, our Tree of Life, directs us to heaven as our first and foundational relationship, and reaches out from there to the world around us with arms outstretched.

Further, it is only through taking up this cross and following our dear lover[3] and LORD, only through laying down our lives to death for the joy set before us, that we can follow Him into the power of resurrection life. The act of laying down everything and not sin management, the power of life released in that act and not judgment of good and evil, these are the Tree of Life to us and in us that will put forth fruit for the healing of the world[4]. We have been perplexed and undernourished because we have been living, serving and eating from a tree that God has brought down, neglecting the tree that will only be our salvation, nourishment and restoration.

---

[1] In this way, "holding to a form of Godliness, yet denying its power." II Tim. 3:5.
[2] I Pt. 1:20; Rev. 13:8.
[3] Luke 9:23.
[4] Again, see Rev. 22:2, esp. leaves and fruit given for healing and sustenance.

To participate with God in His founding of the House of Prayer in this day, then, we must recognize the compost pile of preoccupation with things fallen that we find ourselves in, throw down the fragments of sin management and control that we cling to, and move out toward the grace of the cross embodied in the Tree of Life; full of sustenance and healing. The time is now, and the need is urgent[1]. To do this we've got to throw down our concepts of the North American life we struggle to maintain, we've got to throw down our concepts of church, we've got to throw down our concepts of how the service ought to be, and how we as Christians should operate in "the world". If we don't we will continue to search fruitlessly among the debris of what has been, for a scrap of anything that will sustain us, when the glorious grace and nourishment of God's Tree of Life stands within reach because of the work of Christ's sacrifice for us.

In this pattern for the content of the House of Prayer God is showing us a glimmer of a new approach to life, ministry, and church where all we do becomes a celebration of the grace and mercy of the lamb: the story of God's Love for all of us who are overcoming by the blood of the Lamb[2], the story of the very word of our testimony, and the story of the glory set before us. He is calling us to institute a whole and connected approach where we celebrate the story of God's love for us and what He has done to save us and set us free[3] in three areas: What God has done[4], What God is doing[5], and What God is going to do[6]. We need to bring these stories, which is in reality only one story, together all the time in our faith, life, and practice, and especially as the foundation of the content of the House of Prayer. This brings us to the meaning of the Tree of Life in the vision.

The Three-Strand Cord in the Content of the House of Prayer

---

[1] II Cor. 6:2: NOW is the day of salvation for the Body of Christ in this area.
[2] Rev. 12:11.
[3] Jn. 8:36.
[4] II Cor. 1:10 wonderfully describes this God-ordained structure: "…who [Jesus] delivered us from so great a death…" in the past tense…
[5] II Cor. 1:10: "…and does deliver…" in the present…
[6] II Cor. 1:10: "…in whom we trust that He will yet deliver us…" in the future.

The Tree of Life is a whole made up of three parts, the three-strand cord expressed in the content of the House of Prayer. The roots represent the telling of what God has done in history. This is His story as set down in the Bible, and the story of what He has done for His people throughout the rest of time. This is worship for what God has done. This is the proclamation of the word, not just based on our opinion of a piece of scripture, but an affirmation of the heart of God expressed in the story of what God has done and how He cares for His people. We've got to be grounded in this story, more than in "principles", more than in sermons, and more than in theological treatises[1]. There is a structure to God's story of redemption throughout history, a deep root structure that Christians have largely abandoned since the time of Constantine. We have got to re-connect.

The trunk represents the story of what God has done in our individual lives, and of what He's doing in our lives and the world today. This is an aspect of our celebration that is almost completely absent from our modern North American-style service. It is, however, an absolutely vital and life-giving aspect of God that needs to be celebrated every time we come together. These are our stories unfolding corporately, as well as intercession for others and the world. This is the aspect that bridges and holds together the history of God's faithfulness and the glory to come. Sharing our individual stories corporately, as well as delving in prayer into current events and lifting Him up in praise for His faithfulness to the peoples of the world allows us to draw life[2] from what He's done in history, and helps us connect into what God wants to do among us in the future.

The branches of this Tree of Life represent the story of what we believe God will do in and through us, and from there into the world. This is the sharing and celebration of what He is saying or showing to us. This is prophetic worship. This is the practice of the prophetic, and also the sharing of vision corporately. This is the realm

---

[1] In the same way that Paul did not shrink from declaring the whole purpose of God: Acts 20:27.
[2] These seldom-practiced ways of corporately celebrating the stories of God's work in us today are ways in which we, like Paul in II Pet. 1:12 & 13, can "stir one another up", reminding each other of the truth manifesting in our lives every day.

of growth and change, this is where our healing will come as we learn to hear from God together and begin to set our hearts on His promises[1].

As we throw down what our practice has been under the tyranny of our measurement of the good and the evil, and take up the practice of Life in these three areas we will see the fruit that we have been longing for. Taking up an emphasis on the story of the power of redemption to create in us a new man reaching for a new destiny, we will become connected to our root, and the life we've wanted will flow naturally through that connection instituted in the very fabric of our corporate and personal practice to bring forth the fruit that will be good for sustenance and healing for the nations. We will become strong, healed, and be able to offer healing and sustenance to the world around us. I believe that this kind of focus will become equally necessary for the church in the days ahead, as well as absolutely crucial for the building of the House of Prayer in the earth.

The Deep Roots

If it is true that we have suffered and starved in the partaking of and serving from a collection of scattered and unrelated pieces, then it is true that we need a structural whole as a pattern. Further, we need a congruent set of touchstones, the deep roots, if you will[2], grounded in the story of God's heart for His people to guide us. But what pattern is there? What is the deep root system that we can draw from in our seasons of worship, intercession and revelation?

A clue has been brought back to me through this vision. The clue to the identity of the deep roots of our faith and practice[3] has come to me in the times of flow and blessing we have fitfully enjoyed in the past years. Many times when God seemed to meet us and there was a special flow in our worship and ministry as a church my wife

---

[1] As in II Pt. 1:4.
[2] Ps. 1:2 & 3.
[3] A prophecy of this work is specifically given to Zion, which is a clear picture of the House of Prayer, among other prophetic entities. In this way we are to "...take root downward and bear fruit upward..." Is. 37:31.

and I would marvel at how the songs, words, and messages went along with the seasonal emphasis in God's ancient calendar. This brings us back to one of the central scripture passages describing the work of the founding of the House of Prayer:

> "And foreigners who bind themselves to the LORD to serve Him, to love the name of the LORD, and to worship Him -- all who keep the Sabbath without desecrating it and who hold fast to My covenant -- these I will bring to My holy mountain and give them joy in My House of Prayer. Their burnt offerings and sacrifices will be accepted on My altar; for My house will be called a House of Prayer for all nations" Isaiah 56:6&7.

This passage indicates that foreigners will be brought to the House of Prayer, yes, yet they will be Gentiles who keep the Sabbath, and who hold fast to the covenant God made with His people Israel. This speaks to me of we Gentiles in this day being brought to the task of establishing the House of Prayer, and at the same time being drawn into the spirit and truth of all that God has set forth for His people[1].

I was dissatisfied with santas and bunnies. Dionne was pregnant with our son, Jonah, and I was seeking God as to what kind of heritage I was to practice and hand down to my children. As I pressed into the presence of God with this issue, God told me, "It's in the Book!" As I have searched "the Book" He has opened to me much depth of meaning in the celebrations He ordained for His people as "everlasting ordinances". The seasons of God's calendar revolve around seven commanded festivals. You can find them in Leviticus 23.

These festivals are given to us by God so that we can come into an understanding of the purposes of the Messiah, both in the First Century and in these last days. The spring festivals[2], with the paschal lamb and their culmination in the festival of Pentecost, are a picture of the coming of Jesus as the suffering Messiah[3]: The Lamb of God that

---

[1] John 4:23,24.
[2] Descriptions found in Lev. 23:5-22.
[3] "Let us celebrate the feast..." I Cor. 5:7 & 8.

takes away the sin of the world[1]. The fall festivals[2], beginning with the sudden blowing of the trumpet[3], and culminating in our dwelling with God[4] and celebrating the Word, are a picture of the coming of Jesus as victor and king: the Bridegroom coming for His Bride, the Lion of Judah come to rule and reign. It is a revelation to many believers that God has given His people throughout history a heritage wherein, if we embrace it, our lives become a celebration of the Messiah Jesus -- the lover of our souls!

This is not an appeal to move to a legalistic practice based in old Jewish law. It is a challenge from God to move to a structure for our corporate practice that draws meaning in His way, from His seasons of celebration and remembrance that He has set down for us[5]. The facts are that God instituted His calendar, Jesus lived it, the apostles taught it, and Roman Christianity left it. Further, what other structural root system, what other heritage has God given in His wisdom and love that may give form and meaning to our faith and practice as we step into the fullness of our calling as a priesthood in the earth? What better heritage and structure than the one God has ordained for the benefit of His people throughout time?

The Vision Put Into Practice

The vision of The Tree of Life makes several things clear: We cannot make the practice of the House of Prayer like the traditional

---

[1] John 1:29, Rev.5:9 & 10. It is of astonishing importance to note the framing of the declaration here in Revelations: worthy is the Lamb that was slain (a reference to Jesus, His work, and the absolute foundation of such in God's ancient purposes -- our ancient Jewish roots), purchasing people from every tongue and tribe (a reference to the end-time purpose of the House of Prayer as explored in chapter 2), making those people into a Kingdom of Priests (also explored in Chapter 4 as one of the necessary foundations of the House of Prayer). This passage points strongly to the need for the end-time Church to re-connect with its ancient roots, and also references the House of Prayer in its purpose and structure.
[2] Descriptions found in Lev. 23:23-44.
[3] The Feast of Trumpets foreshadows the trump referred to in I Cor. 15:51, 52.
[4] The Feast of Tabernacles foreshadows Revelation 21:3, 4.
[5] I Cor. 10:11.

service. We cannot make it about a program. We must make it about the story. We can practice this connection in the three-strand cord of His story, our story, and the story of the glory to come throughout our daily lives, and we must connect each of the three parts of the story in creative ways every time we come together. We can make it about the story by proclaiming the narrative of His love for His people through creative worship, active doing, through words, visions, and the prophetic, and through prayer and ministry that is all linked around the story.

In this new vision I hear God saying: "Make it fun[1], make it interactive, make it participatory[2]." Give multiple opportunities using varied methods to tell, respond to, and celebrate the story. Vary our approaches. Use physical object lessons. Use large group methods, or small group story, response, sharing and ministry with one another. Use learning style theory to generate different kinds of approaches. Use active involvement and creative projects at times, with children, youth, and adults participating together. Encourage everyone to take up some sort of creative expression, and tell the story to each other through these. And don't be confined to a building[3]! It seems of particular importance that we are absolutely awash with teachers throughout the body of Christ right now, who understand these kinds of methods, and could implement them. This is no coincidence!

Conclusion

I believe that God is calling the faith and practice represented in the House of Prayer to a content grounded in the work of the cross and the power of grace, in this time when He is preparing to pour out His spirit on all flesh. A shift in emphasis from a theology based in the sinful nature of man to a theology based on the story of the power of redemption to create in us a new man with a new destiny will draw more into a living faith, as well as increase heart interaction and whole person participation. It will cultivate a higher level of community as

---

[1] With Joy as in Is. 56:7.
[2] Supremely participatory as described in Eph. 4:16.
[3] Acts 7:48-50 and Is. 66:1, 2. Was it not God's hand that made the whole earth? Why shouldn't we worship Him in parks, in wilderness, on the streets?

more of us are mentored, blessed, trusted and released to exercise our talents and giftings in corporate worship in the House of Prayer. I believe that God is waiting to pour out His spirit for a structure like this to be built among His people so it can be a platform upon which He can release the outpouring -- and broadcast it forth into the church and the world. To build this kind of faith and practice in the House of Prayer will take absolute dependence upon the leading of the Spirit every step of the way[1]. This is the only way we will be able to birth such a radical vision, and that reliance on the Spirit will be the insurance that it will not bloat into just another programmatic structure.

    We are in the time of the restoration of all things. God is calling His people to the faith and practice that He has intended from the foundation of the world. God is showing us a glimmer of an approach to life and ministry where we celebrate the story of God's Love in and through each of us, in His way, on His calendar. He is calling us, in the establishment of the House of Prayer, to institute a whole and connected approach, an invitation to everyone who wants to join as participants, where we celebrate the story of God's extravagant love[2] for us shown in what He has done, is doing, and will do to redeem us and set us free to establish the Kingdom of God in the earth, operating in the same way that it does in heaven.

---

[1] This is that utter surrender reflected in Romans 8:14.
[2] Eph. 2:4, God's "Great Love".

Section III
The Many Faces of The House of Prayer

Section III
The Therapy Process of the Inner
Prayer

CH 6 The House of Prayer as Bridal Chamber

We are the Bride of Christ. Among us there is "now no Jew nor Greek, no male nor female, no slave nor free[1]"... we are all part of the bride. As such we have a place of unique privilege in His presence. The reasons we don't immediately understand this are simple: The kingdoms of this world are bent on us not conceiving of this simple yet powerful spiritual fact. The truth that we must grasp, in order for the Bride to be made ready in the earth, is that Christ has loved us as He has commanded a husband to love his wife: He laid down His life for us[2]. He is therefore calling us in this day to come to Him as the Lover of our souls[3].

This simple spiritual shift opens up vast new vistas of the meaning of relationship with Christ. Yes, God is my Father. Yes, the Holy Spirit is my friend, guide and teacher. But Jesus is the Lover of my soul. Suddenly every nuance of Song of Solomon has new and highly personal meaning. My heart takes on a new thrill at the thought of coming into His presence. My time with Him takes on new depth and vibrancy. The first step to living out this new understanding, as in any relationship, is to get to know Him in this place of intimacy.

It was years ago, in the early 1980's when Jesus first called me into this kind of intimate depth. At the time I knew God, but was struggling in a deep pit of hurt and bitterness -- trying to meet my inmost needs in any way possible, often self-destructively. I began to have attacks that felt like heart attacks, accompanied by hounding irrational fears. I was 22 years old.

---

[1] Gal. 3:28, also see Col. 3:11.
[2] Eph. 5:32.
[3] Drawing near in full assurance of His love as in Heb. 10:22.

One day I was cleaning a friend's house in order to get by, when I heard my name. I knew who it was; that voice was strong and clear, and full of beckoning. This was my moment of crisis -- I knew I could ignore that voice and run the risk of never hearing it again, or I could respond. I had to respond. As I said, "Yes, LORD..." I could not have predicted what happened next.

A force hit me that was so strong I lost consciousness and fell to the floor. I felt like I was being pounded: like I was under a vast weight that was pounding and pounding over me, around me, in me and through me. I struggled to catch my breath. Soon I began to realize that I was being pounded with wave after rolling wave of pure love, the love of God unleashed on my hurting heart. I relaxed and wept under the crushing weight of God's heart of love for me.

As I started to come to, I began a mental list of all the things in my life that I had to change: no more going to bars, I would have to dump my friends, throw away a lot of stuff. But God stopped me. In that moment with my eyes still wet with the tears of the beauty and crushing glory of His love for me, He told me I couldn't do anything to change my life. He reminded me that I couldn't even live the Christian life by myself. I had tried. In that sweet moment He told me that I couldn't do anything to change myself but two things: stay close enough to hear Him, and when I hear Him, put it into action[1].

Suddenly the futility of religion and centuries of man's efforts became clear to me. That was my moment of truth, and I've been practicing staying close and acting on what the Spirit says to me ever since. From that time I knew that I had to give myself completely to a personal relationship with God -- but even then I had to give up my own efforts and religious notions about what God required. There were only two things I could do -- still myself to hear him, and be obedient to that voice[2].

I propose that we can reach truly outside self not just to experience, but to experience God Himself. I propose that truth is personality, and therefore cannot be comprehended and encapsulated

---

[1] We can see these two foundational precepts in John 10:27 and John 2:5.
[2] Listening and obedient as in Ps. 46:10, I Sam. 15:22, and Is. 1:19.

by mere reason, language, or religious practice. Ultimate Truth is personality in that it has intelligence, awareness, purpose, and a desire to be known. He can be known, not as one knows a subject or set of facts, but only as one knows another personality: through relationship. As opposed to knowing information about someone or something, relationship requires time, successive levels of intimacy, investment of oneself; and in just such a way God may be known.

After my commitment to give myself over completely to this relationship with God, I was left with the question of how I would go about it. Every time I asked Him how I could do it, I was answered, "Wait on the LORD[1]". Over and over I heard those words as I tried to figure out what they meant. I tried to analyze and interpret them, first one way and then another until finally I decided to just take them at face value -- and simply wait.

I waited and waited[2], setting aside time every day. I really didn't know what I was waiting for. Sometimes I prayed, sometimes I sang, but mostly I worked on quieting my heart and thoughts[3] in order to concentrate on God's heart and God's thoughts. I began to become aware of a place inside me -- a still, spacious place where I could feel a faint flickering as if there were a flame deep inside. I learned to include rather than trying to exclude my thoughts, focusing every thought and feeling on this new presence I was becoming aware of.

One day I met Jesus in this place, and realized that this is where He had come to live inside me. I began to come here every day to be with Him, sometimes talking together, but mostly just being together -- touching intimately in this deep place while the flame grew and burned steadier, higher, and brighter. Soon I was taking hours just basking in this newfound intimacy. It got to the point where I was lying in His presence for most of the day, communing deeply in the embrace of His love. He would tell me when it was time to go to work, go shopping or go pay my bills.

---

[1] Ps. 5:3, Ps. 27:14, Ps. 33:20, Ps. 37:7, Ps. 37:34, Ps. 38:15, Ps. 40:1, Ps. 119:166, Ps. 130:5, Ps. 130:6, Prov. 20:22, Is. 8:17, Is. 26:8, Is. 30:18, Is 40:31,Lam. 3:24, Lam. 3:26, Zeph. 3:8.
[2] I waited on God continually, as in Hos. 12:6.
[3] Quietness and trust as in Is. 30:15.

I continue to take time to cultivate this place, this flame, this relationship, but I find now that I can stop anywhere and enter there for peace, strength, and a profound companionship. The strength, healing, and wisdom I enjoy there spills out into every part of my life giving wholeness and new meaning to my marriage, work and friendships.

In waiting on God our heart should be set on Him and not on ourselves, or what we want from Him. This is where the names of God come in handy. We come to Him in quietness so that we can learn what His presence is like. As we still our restless minds and hearts, He is able to awaken our spirits and stir up the childlike heart of trust, dependence, and confidence in Him. Wait on God in expectation; as a living being who knows you and longs to fill you. If you will simply wait on God, He will teach you and work healing, wholeness, and wisdom in your spirit, heart, and mind.

When Esther Approached The King

When Esther approached the king and his scepter was extended toward her it didn't stop there. At that point she prepared a banquet for her lover in the presence of her enemy[1]! Why? Because she could not defeat her enemies by herself. She had to come to her king in dependence. Further, she could not simply reach out in pride and arrogance to take what she wanted from her lover, from her king. She had to come to Him in humility.

We have the ear of the King at this time, but we cannot reach out to take hold of what is ours in Him by our own hand. We must prepare a place for Him; prepare a banquet for the two of us to come together in love and intimacy – even in the midst of our crisis.

Our enemies come as an impetus, as a catalyst that makes us desperate to draw near and receive from the hand of our lover and King! But we cannot receive what He so much wants to give to us by reaching out for it and taking it for ourselves. We must prepare a banquet for our King, a sacrifice of heart, a drawing near to Him in dependence and humility[2]. We must draw near in love, not in

---

[1] From Esther 5:2-4.

manipulation or with a demand.

We can set a banquet for our King in our worship, and by lifting Him up in praise and gratitude. He is worthy of our praise. We can conduct and maintain a banquet for our King by giving Him of our time. Esther didn't make just one banquet for the king. We must spend time in His presence for His presence to become real to us. Spending time with Him is also the only way we will be formed into His likeness. He is worthy of our time.

We can complete that banquet of love by making an offering of our simple obedience to Him. Start with obedience in the small things. Show your heart's devotion by practicing obedience to what He is saying to you right now. Just love Him in simple obedience. He is worthy of our obedience.

What we are talking about here is worshipping Him with everything; everything that we have, everything that we do, and everything that we are. Worshipping Him with our time, talents and obedience makes us into the people that He has always wanted to establish in the earth. Once we have prepared this kind of banquet for the one we love He will be eager to grant us what we need[1], what we want, in fact everything necessary for life and godliness[2].

The Strand of Worship in Everything

Once we have entered into this kind of experience of intimacy with the heart of the Lover of our souls, everything we do and everything we are becomes an expression of worship to the One we love. Many times the simple expressions of our hearts become transformed into breathtaking acts of worship.

One of our main values in the House of Prayer is to express our love and commitment to Jesus by and through every expression of worship that flows through the unique hearts of each team member. We encourage each other to extravagantly return our various talents to

---

[2] Heb. 10:22.
[1] Philip. 4:19.
[2] II Pet. 1:3.

God for the expression of our hearts to Him[1]. In offering our many giftings and talents to God in worship we purpose to:

Enter into the very presence of God.

Minister to the great and loving heart of God through our unique heart expressions.

Encourage and inspire each other corporately to enter into worship.

Give multi-sensory expression to the worship in our hearts, a scripture, a prayer, or the prophetic.

Be well pleasing to the LORD. II Corinthians.5:9

In addition, all worship expressions are tools of intercession and spiritual warfare. It was with singers and trumpets that the Israelites often won their battles: "Let God arise, and His enemies will be scattered[2]".

Areas of Worship Expression

Music- Worship teams provide an atmosphere that is intended to facilitate worship visually, musically and spiritually. This is accomplished through song and the use of various kinds of instruments; from drums to guitars, from keyboards to ethnic percussion instruments. The psalmist encourages us to "Let everything that has breath praise the LORD![3]"

Dance- Worship dance can be any choreographed or spontaneous physical expression of worship[4]. Dance and processions give us a physical release for our hearts, and a physical demonstration of our worship.

Worship dance is found all throughout the Bible. The word

---

[1] Rom. 12:6-8.
[2] Ps. 68:1, Numb. 10:35.
[3] Ps. 150:6.
[4] Ps. 149:3, Ps. 150:4.

dance in Hebrew means to turn, twist, move in the round, skip and leap. Singing and shouting often accompanied dance in biblical times. We find that God's people danced when they were released from bondage in Ex. 15:20, King David danced before the LORD in 2 Sam. 6:14-16, We are commanded to dance in worship in Psalm 149, and the lame man danced when he was healed (Acts 3:8-10).

Flags and Banners- The Bible has many references to "banners", "standards" or "ensigns". All three words as used in the scripture refer to flags and banners. When Moses and the Israelites were victorious over the Amalekites in Exodus 17 Moses calls God by a new name, Jehovah Nissi, which means "the LORD my banner"[1]. Song of Solomon 2:4 tells me that "His banner over me is love".

Flags and banners are used in worship to exalt Jesus and the kingdom of God before men and before the powers of darkness. During worship or ministry time flags proclaim the dominion of God's kingdom and mark our spiritual territory. They are a declaration of our salvation, redemption, healing and the authority we have obtained in the heavens and on earth through the work of Christ. They may also serve to invite and usher in the presence of the Holy Spirit. In flag worship the flag bearer is truly "raising the standard" of spiritual dominion and unity.

Flags are found in scripture:
For warfare in Psalm 74:4, Isiah 31:9, Psalm 20:5 and Song of Songs 6:4.
As a rallying point in Isaiah 11:10.
As a proclamation in Jer. 50:2, 4:6, 51:12, and Isaiah 62:10.

Poetry and Writing- The Bible is a book of poetry, stories and prophetic writing. The Psalms is a book of poetry, Song of Solomon is an excellent example of an epic love poem; the whole bible is ample testimony that the art of writing has a definite place in our worship expression.

We use writing in our worship expression by writing down our thoughts, feelings or visions[2] and then displaying them, reading them

---

[1] Ex. 17:15.
[2] Just as in Ps. 45:1.

aloud, or making a recording of them, often along with music. This book is an example of worship through writing: it was written largely in times of worship and revelation in the House of Prayer. Writing is an important way to communicate our hearts and vision in worship[1].

Visual Art- The visual arts have been a wonderful and rich part of worship expression from the days of Moses to the Renaissance. Architecture, painting, worship implements and stained glass, among other visual expressions, have profoundly enriched man's experience of the worship of God for thousands of years.

From the beginning God has been a God of creativity, "In the beginning, God created…" Gen. 1:1. In Moses' time God commanded the skillful creation of beautiful implements of worship, (Ex 25-28). Jesus must have designed and built furniture as a carpenter in Galilee, and Paul used his creative skills to make his "tents"[2].

We want to release each other and ourselves to create beautiful, unique expressions of our hearts, of scripture, or of what God is showing us in our worship. This kind of expression often results in a powerful communication of the truth or God's presence. Visual art -- including painting, sculpture, video, photography and more -- is an increasingly important avenue of communication in our culture. What better subject matter to portray in the visual arts than our hearts in the worship of the God of creation?

The precious intimacy of the Bridal experience is the very first step in preparing a place, preparing the House of Prayer in our hearts, in the people, in our cities. Cultivating the secret place[3] is a crucial foundation upon which everything else that may become the House of Prayer depends. The intimacy of the bridal chamber must be the basis for our own hearts, for any leadership team, and for any training program in the House of Prayer. There is a House of Prayer where this kind of intimacy is established and cultivated in the presence of the lover of our souls.

The overflow from this place of deep intimacy is the worship

---

[1] If the Athenian poets proclaimed a god they didn't even know, Acts 17:28, how much more should we proclaim the God we know through poetry and writing!
[2] Carpenter Jesus in Mark 6:3, and "tentmaker" Paul in Acts 18:3.
[3] Ps. 91:1.

that forms the first strand of the three-strand cord that is the veritable DNA of the House of Prayer. Whether our worship is enacted through dance, song, or flags, expressed in painting, photography, poetry or books, or vocalized in prayer, proclamation or exaltation, the intimate relationship expressed in Bridal worship stands as a foundational strand in the three-strand cord of the work of heaven, the basis of the House of Prayer.

CH 7 The House of Prayer as Strategy Room

I was at the Wednesday night prayer meeting at our church. God had broken out among us by then in such a big way that our prayer meetings had turned into huge celebrations of worship, prayer and revelation in prophetic words and experiences. This Wednesday night had been very good. We worshipped with song and dancing, enjoyed some soaking in His presence until the spirit of prophecy broke out, with the children prophesying just as much -- or more than -- the adults. Then we began to pray through what The LORD was saying, pray for and prophesy over needs, and pray over each other.

The meeting was winding down and there were just a handful of us left praying over each other and blessing and extolling the LORD. While I basked in the glow of the presence of the LORD, I suddenly stood at the edge of our downtown square. It was night. It was a very vivid experience, as if I were right in the middle of it, seeing, touching and feeling it with all of my senses.

I stood on the edge of the square with a bow in my hands and a quiver of arrows on my back. God said: "Do you want it?"

"What do you want to give me, God?" I asked Him.

"Do you want it?" He immediately asked again. As I looked across the darkened square I began to realize that He meant the very land that I stood upon.

"Is it Courthouse Square that you want to give me?" I asked, a little overwhelmed.

"Do you want this land?" He asked with joy and love and insistence. I quickly replied,

"Yes, LORD, I want it!"

"Then take it!" He eagerly enjoined. With His command to take the land I knew that I was to shoot an arrow into the ground as a claim, a standard, a marker that would mark the territory as mine. I eagerly pulled an arrow from the quiver-full on my back, strung it on my bow, and shot the arrow into the ground at the corner of the square. As my arrow flew I saw that it was an arrow with a tip of flame. As the flaming arrow came firmly to rest in the ground, many hundreds of arrows flew into place and stuck fast like dominoes falling all around the perimeter of the square. The outline of the downtown square filled with the light of the hundreds of flaming arrows and the light shone down the streets surrounding the square in every direction.

Next I saw two other squares, Railroad Square and Julliard Park, both in the downtown area of Santa Rosa. God asked me if I wanted them as well. I shot arrows into those parcels as I had done at Courthouse Square. They lit up with an outline of flaming arrows whose light shone out down the streets to connect with the others.

Then I was raised up a hundred feet or so into the air. From this vantage point I could see my rented house to the west, and the two on either side that families of friends rented and lived in. The voice of The LORD called out, "Do you want these"?

"Yes LORD!" I shouted as I shot three arrows into the land the homes stood upon. They lit up with a perimeter outline of flaming arrows, sending light down the streets in every direction.

At this point I was raised up high into the sky above the city, where I saw to the north a large fortress with walls and spires of light. It had an emerald rainbow encircling it, giving it the appearance of a shining city of emerald. The LORD called out once more:

"Do you want it?"

"Yes, LORD – I want it!" I cried with joy as I shot arrows into the foundation of the gleaming city. In joyful abandon to His breathtaking call I shot lines of arrows into the main thoroughfares connecting the squares, the homes, and the New Jerusalem established in my city. The thoroughfares lit up in a huge triangle that illuminated the whole region, and I saw a great traffic of travelers and supplies moving on the thoroughfares of light between the squares, homes and the glorified church.

As I hung high over the city, laughing and howling in ecstasy and victory, a voice like a great booming chorus of many voices began to shout out:

"I give you the Three of the Three – the three of the street, the three of the home, and the three of the church! I give you the Three of the Three!" Over and over again that voice reverberated through my being, as I gradually became aware of the room around me and my friends quietly praying for one another.

Still half in a haze, and charged with the power of that great voice, I leapt to my feet shouting: "He's giving me the Three of the Three! He's giving me the Three of the Three!"

"What?" everyone stared with blank stares. "What are you talking about?" I tried to clear my head as I struggled to put the experience into words. My halting account of the spiritual journey I had just been on threw everyone into sudden responses. Some fell down onto the floor, while many started to prophesy spontaneously concerning what I was struggling to tell.

Since that time I have realized much about the meaning of this experience. The Three of the Three is not about me. It is about the authority that God is ready to give to communities of His people as they establish the House of Prayer in their midst. The threefold cord of Worship, Intercession and Revelation – the work of heaven itself— contains power to transform our public squares, our homes, and our churches, even to establishing the very New Jerusalem in our midst. The House of Prayer established in the midst of the street, the home and the church is an establishment of Love, Justice and Righteousness in our community as worship, intercession and revelation is founded twenty-four hours a day in the heart of our cities. In the establishment of the House of Prayer, the body, soul and spirit of the streets, the body, soul and spirit of the home and the body, soul and spirit of the church can become radically transformed -- becoming the City of God coming down out of heaven[1], and established in the earth. All of this will happen if we want it – and if we will stake our claim in our cities to establish the House of Prayer in the earth. Do you want it?

The Strategic Power of the House of Prayer

Worship, intercession and revelation are strategic arrows of

---

[1] Found in Rev. 21:2.

fire in the hands and mouths of the priesthood, just waiting to be let fly to transform our cities. When intercession and worship are intricately woven together they create a powerful force that can push back darkness and provide a space of spiritual safety. Intercession can break us through into higher and deeper places with God, while revelation shows us where and how to move, and worship moves us into those new areas through the power of the exaltation of the throne of God. The simplest definition of intercession is "to go between", or to "stand in the gap". Intercession is the ability to help carry another's burden in prayer, to stand between the people of God and the opposing enemy in prayer, or to break through the chains that are holding back a person, region or nation[1]. Intercession has the power to cause a breaking through into the heavenly realm, creating a clear space so that worship can do its job of enthroning Jesus, opening the door to revelation bringing us face to face with God's Kingdom come and His will being done in the earth. Only when intercession paves the way, only then can mercy and justice flow forth into the streets of our cities.

Let's take our cities as an example of what the House of Prayer is called to do in intercession. We can see in the word that God has a heart for cities[2]. In fact, God's heart for cities seems to be at the core of His plan to establish His Kingdom reign throughout the earth. Jesus said:" ...you will be my witnesses in Jerusalem, and in all Judea and Samaria, and to the ends of the earth" Acts1:8. He wants to empower us to take our cities, and this work must start in prayer, and be accomplished in acts of intercession.

Our cities, however, are such as they are in their darkness and violence, or mere self-indulgence and indifference, because they are built on faulty spiritual foundation stones. The beliefs, purposes and deeds that went into the founding of our cities established these physical cities as physical and spiritual entities. These beliefs, purposes and deeds formed the foundation stones upon which our cities are founded; whether foundation stones of righteousness or unrighteousness.

---

[1] All according to Gal. 6:2.
[2] God's heart for cities may be seen in Jonah 4:11 and Is. 66:10-14, as well as many other accounts.

Our cities are the way they are because of the influences of the foundations upon which they were built. It has been seen in many cities, that racial tensions are built on foundations of prejudice and wrongdoing against minority groups. Sexual trade, whether in prostitution or adult entertainment stores, may very well be built on foundations of historic lasciviousness and disrespect of women. These are just some possible examples given to show the deeper spiritual causes of many of our societal ills. We as Christians pray against the towers or landmarks of sin and darkness that are obvious in our city's landscape, and wonder why we are not effective. The reason we are not as effective as we would like to be is that these visible signs of darkness are just manifestations of deeply embedded foundation stones laid at the inception of our municipality, or somewhere during its growth and development. For a more complete examination of this spiritual dynamic and the role of intercession for our cities, there are a number of good books. Just two possibilities are John Dawson's book, <u>Taking Our Cities for God</u>, or <u>Releasing Heaven On Earth</u>, by Alistair Petrie.

So we understand that our cities are built on faulty foundation stones, as well as good ones. What are we to do about it? Some may want to ignore faulty foundation stones, trying to focus on the positive and build toward the good using what is at hand. The problem with this approach, one that has been popular for a very long time, is that unless The LORD builds the house, we labor in vain to see any good accomplished[1]. The foundation stones of darkness and sin will shift under the weight of anything built upon them, influencing and shaping the effort until the whole structure is unusable and unsafe.

Others have tried to break down the faulty foundations in their cities with much fervent prayer, effort and expense: lobbying for change, picketing, attempting to introduce new legislation, starting foundations, backing politicians, running campaigns, and on and on. I can applaud the efforts of these tireless men and women, but I haven't seen much real change in a community toward genuine righteousness resulting from these kinds of political efforts. We don't want to build

---

[1] Ps. 127:1.

new legislative agendas on the old, faulty foundations, any more than we want to break apart the foundations of our cities with prayer campaigns or political offensives merely intended to tear down apparent problems.

The word tells us that our enemies are not political structures or flesh and blood opponents, but "...powers and principalities in heavenly places"[1]. The word also says that our weapons are potent, and capable of tearing down spiritual strongholds. But what are these spiritual weapons, and how do we use them?

The command of God to Moses was:"...gather the assembly together. Speak to that rock before their eyes and it will pour out its water. You will bring water out of the rock for the community..."[2]. This is what we are to do to preserve our communities: we must recognize the false spirit, the power or principality behind the faulty foundation stones in our communities, and speak to them in the authority we have in Christ. To pray effectively for our cities we must take up the staff of our authority. We must gather with like-minded brothers and sisters[3]. Even with the staff of our authority in Christ in our hands, we must take care to not strike out in our own strength, or the heat of our anger[4]. We must speak to the rock, breaking the power of the false foundation precepts.

We must then go one step further. We must identify God's purposes for those individual foundation stones and speak, pray and prophesy these purposes into the foundations of our cities. We know that if we drive out one spiritual stronghold but do not fill that place with the Spirit of God and His purposes, we will find that place taken by seven more spiritual strongholds, and even darker than before[5]. So we must identify God's kingdom purpose in the foundation stones of our communities and pray these purposes into existence. Brought into God's purposes in this way, foundation stones of prejudice become foundations of a heart of love and acceptance, even a heart of

---

[1] Eph. 6:12.
[2] Num. 20:7, 8.
[3] As in Phil. 2:2.
[4] We may not react like Moses in Num. 20:11.
[5] Matt. 12:43-45, Luke 11:24-26.

evangelism for the nations of the world. Foundations of sexual promiscuity can be transformed into foundations of a new passion for the lover of our souls. When the foundation stones of our cities come into the purposes God has intended for them, the new foundation our community is built upon becomes an altar to God. Upon that altar God will send the fire of His presence. It is in this fire that our cities will be transformed.

There are many ways we can pray and live out this kind of intercession. Intercessory acts, simple acts done in response to the leading of the Holy Spirit, can be powerful ways to enact the will of God in the earth. Identificational intercession[1] -- identifying so closely with a group or another person in prayer that we can enter into repentance, forgiveness or an intercessory act on their behalf -- can be a bridge to bringing the power of that act into reality for the one prayed for.

Praying the Bible and Proclamation of what God says in His word is an age-old spiritual practice that has been effective through the ages for Jews, monks and saints since before the time of Christ. Praying from the throne, a positioning of ourselves in prayer from our place as seated with Christ in heavenly places at the right hand of the Father[2], has become the most awesome and effective prayer that I've found in my life. Birthing -- praying out the groanings that are beyond words[3] -- is another powerful place in prayer. The creativity of God is limitless in showing us new ways to pray through and live out our intercession. Further, whether it is enacted through dance, song, or flags, published in articles, poetry or books, or vocalized in the many expressions of prayer, the three-strand cord of worship, intercession and revelation in the House of Prayer is key to the transformation of our cities in these last days.

---

[1] The basis for this can be seen in John 20:23.
[2] As in Eph. 2:5, 6.
[3] As described in Rom. 8:26, 27.

CH 8 The House of Prayer as Creative Community

The Need for Creative Community

Human beings are complex organisms[1], and as such no one-size-fits-all spiritual approach will ever be truly effective for the majority of people. This is especially true for those who are poor, broken, hurting, or in some other way disenfranchised from the mainstream. We are in a time where God is shaking the world and the church[2]; He is emphasizing the value of the least[3], and making us aware of our need for change. We see our need, yet solutions elude us because they lay outside our systems and structures and programs. The answer lies in His heart, and what His heart created us for as human beings.

In the beginning, God created[4]. This is the first manifestation of God that we see in the word, indeed the first role He shows Himself playing. I believe that this is so for good reason: the creative God is fundamental to who He is. God is love, and He creates out of that heart of love, for the purposes of love. God is the supreme creator. What's more, He created us in the same image[5]. Humans are created first to find ourselves in the love of our Creator. We are then made with a need and a call to uniquely express our love in return to Him, and as an overflow, express that love to those around us. As this love flows

---

[1] We are all "fearfully and wonderfully made" Psalm 139:14.
[2] Heb. 12:25-27; I Pet. 4:17.
[3] A study on the power of the least is a whole book in itself. Some central passages are Matt. 11:11, Luke 9:48.
[4] Gen. 1:1.
[5] Gen. 1:27.

out, we are created to express this love through passionate, creative and practical expressions based on our unique gifts and callings.

In this light, the necessity of addressing the static, passive, mechanized model of religious practice is very urgent in our society. Much current practice of traditional church models amount to little more than spectator events, and the hip, non-traditional and "seeker sensitive" models have largely only resulted in updated, culturally relevant versions of the same old spectator model of church. I say this with the utmost respect to everyone who is honestly pursuing a relationship with God within the bounds of structures like these, and even with a good deal of empathy. I have myself pushed toward a clarity and honesty of relationship with the Lover of my soul through the traditions and assumptions and political structures of church systems from conservative Baptist roots through Assemblies of God, and on into The Vineyard and independent churches. My experience tells me that the fault does not lie with the church; it lies in our very small conceptions of what spiritual life should be. This is why God is raising up Houses of Prayer in our midst as creative communities – bridges to the very life and work of heaven.

The House of Prayer is fundamentally and uniquely equipped to operate in the function of this new connecting structure. It is a model of a new paradigm, a paradigm that focuses on God as the source and the goal of our faith and practice, begins to network individuals and community entities in love and commitment to one another, recognizes and nurtures the image and expression of God that He has created in each one of us, and brings into the earth the very practice of heaven[1]. The House of Prayer, then, can act as a resource for established structures, a connecting force, and a catalyst for positive change.

Clues to the Heart of the New Jerusalem

In pioneering the House of Prayer we have seen the need to structure our efforts within the context of community, and have made

---

[1] Matt. 6:10; Luke 11:2.

steps to teach and implement that value. We have seen the need for a plurality of leadership in order to relieve our reliance on a man, to turn our reliance to the working of the Holy Spirit in each one, and to promote the value and workings of community on every level.

In our practice we have caught the fire of worship, and realize our efforts must be based in a heart of worship of God alone. We have recognized the need for intercession and prayer, for every step must come directly out of our intimate relations with Him. We have recognized our utter need for Him in strength and guidance, and have cultivated hearing hearts that listen and look for the revelation of His heart and mind every step of the way.

All of this flies in the face of our independent, individualistic society that puts a premium on individual power, resources and accomplishment. Jesus, however, makes it very clear that the Kingdom of God is quite unlike our individualistic, hoarding, hierarchical western cultural structures. In fact, it is clear in the scriptures that the societal values that cause us to desire personal power over others, large stores of resources dedicated to our own personal desires and comfortable personal lives set up like individual kingdoms, are reflections of the kingdoms of this world, and not the Kingdom of our God.

We live in a day, thankfully, that the kingdoms of this world are becoming the Kingdom of our LORD, and of His Christ[1]! We know, further, that as we let go of our own kingdoms and let Him begin to radically take charge, He will reign from these places forever and ever! In these last days, this may well be a literal promise beginning to be fulfilled.

In short, Love in the form of interdependent community and utter reliance upon Jesus form the crux that is and always will be the foundation of any structure, form or practice that we can build or take up if we are interested in furthering the Kingdom of God in our lives and in the world around us. We must continue in this foundation, and press in deeper as we go, for our intimacy with Him is the source and the life of anything that we can do. Pursuing this foundation has

---

[1] As in Rev. 11:15.

allowed us to recognize more of what this new Kingdom paradigm may look like.

Based on a community structure, and with an utter focus on God Himself in practice, general outlines of a new paradigm begin to emerge. Personally, God has asked me if I am willing to "learn the new song"[1]. He has asked me if I would be willing to see and walk out the new community-based structure that He has designed. He has also asked me: "Wouldn't I be behind this plan that I and my people develop together?" The purpose of this Writing, then, is to propose a vision for a new community-based entity that takes on by its cooperative structure and complete focus on God, an identity as a House of Prayer. The further purpose is to begin to open the door to exploration and articulation of a new body life based on a new vision, and new ideals.

The Vision

During intercession I had to grab my notebook and start jotting things down in order to clear my mind and focus on God. I jotted down things to remember, a floor plan for a building I didn't know, an odd list of guidelines for living in community, some seeming stray and unconnected statements from the LORD, including a cryptic "Don't worry about the flying monkeys."

Then He planted in my mind a concept of "invitations" based vaguely on a radical new concept in the field of education, yet much magnified and applied to the workings of a community of people. In this concept multiple opportunities to engage in fellowship, worship, intercession, teaching and revelation are operating simultaneously all over a facility that is always open.

Suddenly I saw this place in a visionary way, walked in the front door, and into a roomy foyer where people were talking, sharing, praying together and fellowshipping at tables in a café area. Across the foyer were tables with three or four computers apiece built into their surfaces, where people were involved with interactive computer slide

---

[1] The word commands us to "sing a new song" not just in worship, but in all aspects of our lives: Psalm 33:3, Psalm 96:1, Psalm 98:1, Psalm 144:9.

shows, simple games and websites. The room was hung with art like a gallery throughout, with beautiful and whimsical pieces of sculpture here and there. The walls were painted in blocks of contrasting muted colors, and there was a huge Plexiglas dome overhead.

There were flying monkeys like the ones in the movie, "The Wizard of OZ" flying down at the dome, hitting hard and sliding slowly off in a comical way. Then I remembered the "random" statement, "Don't worry about the flying monkeys". I knew that this meant that this place enjoyed unprecedented protection from attack, but I also started to realize that all this was somehow connected.

I went through the double doors of a large amphitheater where a worship band was playing and a large crowd was worshipping God together. I knew that worship went on here, almost exclusively, all the time. I went back through the door out into the foyer again, and noticed a sign that had a schedule of ongoing events. There was a discussion group in one room, an expressive arts workshop going on in another, alternating drama and short messages on another stage, storytelling with different storytellers and puppeteers in another room, and multimedia video productions being shown in another theater.

There was a room that was long and narrow, with comfortable chairs and couches at odd angles down the middle. The long walls on either side were of chalkboard material, and prayer requests were written all down one side. Anyone with a prayer need could come in here and write their need on the wall, and anyone with a desire to pray could come in here and pray the walls. The facing long wall was covered in answers to the prayers that had once been on the other side. The place was packed with people in the rooms, engaged in all this, and also circulating from opportunity to opportunity. I could see that this was all based on expressions of worship in all of these different media. Leaders were leading in dance worship, video worship, computer worship, musical worship, painting, drawing, and sculpture as worship, theater as worship, worshipping God in writing, photography, teaching, discussion, and on and on. The participants were of all ages; young children, youth and adults working, worshiping, playing, and sharing side-by-side. This place seemed to be a magnet for believers and non-believers, regular participants and newcomers from off the street. This was the House of Prayer!

Once I came out of the vision I started listing what I saw there quickly, in order not to lose it. As I listed, I realized that all this was supported and generated by a community of believers actively engaged in pursuing the creative and practical expressions of the love of God that was unique to each one. I realized that individuals and small groups of people were pursuing their passion and vision and joy throughout the week in ongoing worship, intercession and revelation, in production teams who in turn taught classes which went on day and night, which for their part contributed to the worship, intercession and revelation at this community center that was the center of this community.

I realized that this place had to be equipped with studio space, workshop space, theater and production facilities, and I started to fill in the details and names of the spaces as I realized that the floor plan I had drawn out was a diagram of this building. At this point I knew that every part all made up a whole; notes for a new paradigm of community and worship and outreach to the world.

Leadership

This is going to take team planning and team leadership. I see a leadership team made up of the leaders of different areas of corporate expression, both traditional and creative. A music team leader, a visual art team leader, a drama team leader, a video production team leader, dance team leaders, writers, evangelists, healers, etc. alongside leaders of teams with more traditional roles like technical support and administration. I see leaders of the varied expression teams coming together to discuss the current story God is speaking, coming up with ways to include personal stories, international prayer needs, and victories of the Kingdom that tie in, and brainstorming telling, sharing, and doing methods that would communicate the particular story well while involving the people.

It's possible that everyone who is known as a part of the community could fill out a short sheet that has particulars of their personal story, so the planning group can approach people to share in their own creative way at times when their personal story may be pertinent in some way to the larger story. Then these people could go back to their studios and create, also work with the people involved on their creative expression teams, and students in their workshops to produce materials, art, visuals, media, music, etc. that will be used to frame the streams of worship, intercession and revelation coming forth. Leaders of sessions would be necessary to coordinate the varying aspects to be included; encouraging, ordering, facilitating the flow of the experience.

      This sounds complicated -- like it would be a big production, and it would undoubtedly be that way at times -- but I see it flowing pretty simply and naturally most of the time. A theme taken from God's seasonal calendar at the time, informed by what God seems to be doing in the community and peoples' lives, taken up by varying modes of expressive arts with room for intercessory, prophetic and other spontaneous expressions, can be smoothly coordinated into an interactive celebration of the story of God's love for His people yesterday, today and forever[1].

      I see small task teams formed around interest area, function, talent or skill. All of the teams may not have a focus that is an area of recognized creative expression. They may be technical geniuses or gifted in office management. This is desirable, however, because everyone does not see themselves as creative, expressive people. These will, in time, become creative groups as God expands our concept of creative gifting. Of course everyone has a creative gifting[2], even if it's in the area of accounting! As a community, we need ALL of the gifts in operation. At first the small task teams may take the form of focus groups, for the purpose of discussing the need, the call in an area of interest, and brainstorming possible implementation for the individual body and the community at large. These groups must be brought past the point of planning and discussion, however, every individual must be cultivated and released into personal expression of the heart of Christ in them.

---

[1] Jesus and the story of His love are the same in any format or medium Heb. 13:8.
[2] Rom. 12:4-8.

Implications of a New Practice

The implications of the vision of the House of Prayer as creative community are staggering. This vision gives me hot and cold shivers, both for its breathtaking beauty and its impossibility. For us alone this is impossible, but with God all things are possible[1]! This is not a vision that one person can carry alone, much less make happen. This convinces me that it must be birthed and pursued in the context of community with each member catching a vision for his and her part, and then building it in cooperation with the whole, with extensions into the body at large.

This value of community must extend to the whole body of Christ in a city or region. The churches must "own" the House of Prayer, whether by overall participation or individual leadership of sessions. The House of Prayer can also be an invaluable resource to every church and ministry in the area, and a dynamic outreach to the community at large. It will take concentrated prayer and commitment. It necessitates the articulation and adoption of new values to build, as well as radically new practices. It will take a commitment of heart, time, and resources to each individual mode of expression that comes forth from the heart of the community as God reveals these expressions through us.

It seems clear that it cannot happen all at once; it will take time, more prayer than seems possible, much work, and a mountain of resources. But God has filled me with a conviction that He wants to do it, and He will accomplish it[2]. I am committed to pray and work to see it come to reality, in whatever form He directs, and whatever form the community brings forth.

The House of Prayer as creative community will add to the impetus for meaningful change within the body of Christ, as well as offer practical ideas and solutions based on a new practice. The format

---

[1] Matt. 19:26; Mk. 9:23; Mk. 10:27.
[2] There are many references in which God promises to do this end-time re-establishment, such as II Kings 19:31; Is. 9:7; Is. 44:28. These can be taken as personal promises that He will accomplish this: Rom. 4:21; I Thess. 5:24.

has a relevancy both to our increasingly media-oriented culture, and to the church's call to authentic expression of the love of God. The expressions, over time, will be of increasing quality and relevance, which will generate a demand and subsequently a support for the ongoing pursuits of the community. More importantly, people will be released like never before to give themselves to the love of their Creator in many forms, to seek out what their own unique expression of that love is, and to communicate it in one or more of many emerging forms. The spiritual life of individuals, the specific community, and the civic community as a whole will be deeply impacted by this new practice of multiple creative and practical expressions of God's love for us, and our resulting love for each other. The establishment of the House of Prayer as creative community at any level has the practical potential of re-animating the church to her vital role of light and salt in the world.

CH 9 The House of Prayer as Body Resource Center

The House of Prayer is an effort of the whole Body of Christ. As a work of priestly teams bringing together the different functions of heaven, it becomes a work that must draw together the different characteristics of the whole Body of Christ in a region. On a practical level this is necessary. The mobilization of worship and prayer 24 hours a day seven days a week will take more than any single ministry can muster. But there are deep spiritual reasons that the work of the House of Prayer must be the work of the Body at large in a city or area. The House of Prayer is a key part of the fulfillment of the prayer of Jesus in Matthew chapter seventeen.

Further, as the House of Prayer begins to function as a work of the whole body, it begins to function as a valuable resource to local churches and ministries, and a much needed resource to the body of Christ at large. As these roles of unity and resource for the people of God grow and begin to bear fruit, the House of Prayer becomes a source of truth and life that flows to the city and to the world. To illustrate much of this we'll look at what the Spirit showed to me on a recent trip to a small town.

A Trip to Lillooet

On the 29th of April, 2004, I traveled to Lillooet, a picturesque town nestled in the mountains of north central British Columbia, with a team of guest ministers. We were going in order to pray for the town and the surrounding area, and to reach out with the love of Christ to some of the First Nations youth on a nearby reservation.

It is astonishingly beautiful there. To get out to the reservation we took a narrow gage train from Lillooet back up into high mountain reservation lands. We stayed in a cabin at the edge of a turquoise lake fed by glacier melt from high snow-capped peaks that surrounded us on all sides. The forest runs down to the water, filled with lilac bushes growing wild, which were at the time in full bloom. The mountain cliffs are made of jade. I couldn't have imagined such a rich and beautiful land.

We saw bear, mountain goats, beaver, grouse; the lilac bushes were full of butterflies that all flew up around us as we hiked through the forest. We hiked, fished, canoed around the incredible turquoise lake, and basked in the sun on the lakeshore... Oh, and we worshipped, shared stories, and prayed with small groups of late teen and twenty-something native youth as we roasted weenies around a blazing bonfire. I'm still stricken by the way the moon rose up behind the glacial peaks and shone over the lake.

After our arrival in Lillooet we were walking and praying down the main street of town as we explored some of the shops and picked up some groceries. As I prayed quietly on the sidewalk in the middle of town I felt the presence of spiritual principalities as though they were bending down in hostility from the mountain tops all around[1]. My reaction was not fear because I know that the God who lives in us is much more powerful than those that try to rule over us in this world[2]. I merely took note that the enemy of our souls was overplaying his hand. This is a good sign that the Spirit of God has plans to do something mighty, and that our enemy is concerned. Also, in this overreaction there may be clues to the spiritual strongholds that hold temporal sway in the area. I was able, in that moment, to discern spirits of depression, anguish, suspicion and separation, and bondage to darkness that keeps men and women blind to the light and works of the Spirit of God[3].

So right there we have a preliminary prayer outline, a line-up of topics resident within the community that can be targeted with the light of love. The first order of business is not to charge in with prayer and spiritual warfare, however. The first thing to do when we find ourselves facing the darkness is to simply turn on the light[4]. Our first

---

[1] As in Eph. 6:12.
[2] I John 4:4.
[3] This last spiritual condition is outlined in II Cor. 4:4.
[4] Eph. 5:13.

order of business is to lift up the rulership of the God of the universe. We must begin by acknowledging His absolute rulership in our lives, walking it out, and by lifting up His power and might over us and over the earth in worship. We must gather to lift His power and might up over the land with abandoned worship, proclamation and the proclamation of His word. Worship is our first and most potent spiritual weapon. Let God arise, and His enemies will be scattered[1]!

Therefore, after I felt this spiritual hostility and paused to sense what I could get from The Lord in it, I began to softly lift up His Name. I quietly sang His praise and proclaimed His power and might while standing on the sidewalk in the middle of the main street in Lillooet. Immediately I saw the mountains becoming mountains of The Bride. I saw pure white bridal veils cascading down into the valley around me. I saw the moon smiling down with a terrific light that flooded the valley[2]. I began to speak this out in agreement with the Spirit of God, and in proclamation of this truth He was showing me. Bridal veils and the moon both being symbolic of the Bride of Christ, I believe that a great key to the work of the power of the gospel of Christ going forth in Lillooet and the surrounding areas is the Bride of Christ coming together to "arise and shine[3]", and lift up His rulership and reign. It seems, then, that worship is a key. Prayer is also a key, and a coming together of the Body simply to worship and lift up His name is key to turning on the light in Lillooet.

Later we hiked up on the bluff by the airport, and we prayed over the city. As we stood together praying I saw a huge eagle rise up from the city and fly up into the sky. As soon as the eagle disappeared into heaven a huge dove fell down upon the city. I feel that if we are able to accept, love and give place to the indigenous people of the land, even though their culture may look different from ours, they will rise up as worshippers and intercessors – eagle warriors – and bring forth a mighty outpouring of the Spirit of God over the land. There is a strong connection between this land and the people of this land. God is

---

[1] Psalm 68:1.
[2] In ancient Hebrew typology, the moon is symbolic of the beloved depicted in Song of Songs, a depiction of the Bride of Christ!
[3] As in Is. 60:1.

giving us an opportunity to serve this people in ways that allows them to step up into their destiny; and the destiny of the land will spring forth.

First – Proclaim the awesome greatness of The LORD over the land and its peoples. Lift up His rulership and authority in worship, in proclamation of the word, and in the speaking forth of His praise that the Holy Spirit brings to your lips. Proclaim His Name in worship. Proclaim His Name in native tongues. Proclaim His greatness in the tongues of the people of the land. Shout out His greatness! Dance out your expression of His rulership over the land! Dance as you proclaim His Name, His dominion, His sovereignty in this valley[1].

Next – pray through the breaking down of walls. Pray the preparation of the Bride here. Pray connection and unity among the church, healing and unity between fathers and children, healing and reconciliation between the white and the First Nations peoples, and the healing of injustice over the land. I will say it again: there is a strong connection between this land and the people of the land. Serve this people to step up to their destiny and the destiny of the land will spring forth.

Prophesy to the Mountains!

God began to speak to me in prayer over Lillooet, "Prophesy to the mountains… Prophesy to the mountains". I turned in response to Ezekiel 36:1 "Son of man, prophesy to the mountains of Israel and say, 'O mountains of Israel, hear the word of the LORD". This is a powerful message all by itself. I heard the Spirit of God speaking to the mountains of Lillooet: "Hear the word of the LORD"! I speak to the mountains of Lillooet: "Hear the word of the LORD"! I encourage the people of God in Lillooet to begin saying to the mountains of Lillooet: "Hear the word of the LORD!" … and start speaking the word of God into the land. The mountains of Lillooet, the high places of Lillooet, the powers and principalities of Lillooet: "Hear the word of the LORD"!

This scripture passage pertaining to Lillooet goes further: "This

---

[1] Psalm 32:7; 47:1; 103:19;

is what the Sovereign LORD says: 'The enemy said of you, 'Aha! The ancient heights have become our possession.'" The enemy of our souls thinks he has Lillooet all wrapped up. The enemy thinks that he has taken possession of the mountain heights, the reservation lands, the town and all its people.

But God has a different perspective. God says in verse 11 that "I will increase the number of men and animals upon you, and they will be fruitful and become numerous. I will settle people on you as in the past and will make you prosper more than before. Then you will know that I am the LORD. ^{12} I will cause people, my people Israel, to walk upon you. They will possess you, and you will be their inheritance; you will never again deprive them of their children". God says that He will cause the mountains of Lillooet to know that He is God! He will do this by causing His people to possess the high places that the enemy has thought were his.

This is good news for the land, for God's people, even for people who don't know God, especially the First Nations people – this is good news for everyone that lives in the whole area. God is going to turn on the light, take back the high places, and give the land to His people! He is going to prosper your land more than ever before in order to show everyone who He is, and show the heart of love and compassion that He has for all of the people of Lillooet and the surrounding areas.

There is, however, one important reason He is going to do this. The reason God gives in verse 21 is key to the whole work. "I had concern for my holy name, which the house of Israel profaned among the nations where they had gone." God says that, like the Israelis before us, the people of God have historically profaned His name among the people of the land -- the First Nations people. The Hebrew people did this by taking on the religions of those people. We have done this by our harsh and cruel treatment of these.

God continues, however, in verse 22: "Therefore say to the house of Israel, 'This is what the Sovereign LORD says: It is not for your sake, O house of Israel, that I am going to do these things, but for the sake of my holy name, which you have profaned among the nations where you have gone." God says that it is not for the sake of His people that

He will use them to heal this land. There is unfinished business in the land. The white people who professed knowledge of God did not live out God's love for the First Nations people. With their injustices they have profaned the Name of the LORD. God goes further: "I will show the holiness of my great name, which has been profaned among the nations, the name you have profaned among them. Then the nations will know that I am the LORD, declares the Sovereign LORD, when I show myself holy through you before their eyes". God says that He will change the heart of the church and show His true heart to the First Nations people through them. This will only come about through a coming together of the church in prayer, repentance and ultimately in acts of repentance and restoration between the peoples. But be encouraged, because God says that He will accomplish this great work through you: "...I the LORD have spoken and I will do it[1]"!

I shared this scripture with our team as we gathered after dinner to pray, and immediately one of my friends saw a picture of a huge angel standing over Lillooet. The angel threw down a huge spear that stuck fast, upright in the valley floor. As it stood there in the midst of the valley the lance turned into a double-edged sword[2]. This picture is an encouraging word to Lillooet that God will establish His word in this place[3], and it is a word of confirmation that the truth of Ezekiel 36 will be driven firmly into the heart of this region.

Strategy for Lillooet

All of these pictures, words and scriptures agree and confirm a strategy for establishing the Kingdom of God in Lillooet, or in many other towns and cities across the Northwest, in a greater and more dramatic way than ever before. The strategy is a plan of lifting up the rule and reign of Christ, which will open the door to reconciliation and healing: within the Body of Christ, within families, between white and native peoples, and throughout the land. This will spark a wave of redemption that will result in many saved all across the local

---

[1] Is. 36:36.
[2] Heb. 4:12.
[3] Is. 55:11.

communities. If, then, the established church community can serve the native peoples to begin to take up God's destiny for their lives, the destiny of the entire area will begin to come forth. The answer is healing, and I think that the destiny may well involve healing on a much broader scale.

– Worship is the very first and most critical key to turning on the light. Lift Jesus high over the land and its peoples. Proclaim the awesome greatness of The LORD, lift up His rulership and authority in worship, in proclamation of the word, and in the speaking forth of His praise that the Holy Spirit brings to your lips. Proclaim His Name in native tongues. Proclaim His greatness in the tongues of the people of the land. Dance out your expression of His rulership over the land! Dance as you proclaim His Name, His dominion, His sovereignty in this valley.

-Prayer is central to the whole redemptive progression. Individuals who have a heart for the city must begin to pray for the area.

-The next key is connection. Individuals from any and every group that claims the name of Christ must be called together, given space and time to pray. Connection to outside groups that will commit to relationship, prayer, sharing resource and seeing this process through may also be a critical need. The peoples and ministries of the city shouldn't have to walk alone.

-Pray the preparation of the Bride here. Pray connection and unity among the church. Pray healing and unity between fathers and children, mothers and daughters and extended family. Pray healing and reconciliation between the white and the First Nations peoples. Pray healing of injustice over the land. A prayer center in a neutral space might be helpful.

-The next step will be walking your prayers out with lives of reconciliation and restoration. There is no need to try to make it happen in our own strength, however: God has said that He will do it[1]. That's the great thing; God has said that He will do it. God will fulfill His promises to you if you will pray and let Him take the lid off of

---

[1] I Thess. 5:24!

your lives, your churches, your communities, and fill them with His light[1].

The House of Prayer as Body connection

This example illustrates how the House of Prayer can make a difference in a community. It also shows one of the primary aspects of the House of Prayer: it must be a corporate effort, taken up by the Body of Christ as a whole – at least a good portion of local churches and ministries must be willing to lend support or be directly involved. The House of Prayer takes on the local character of the people of God in an area as more groups and churches become involved. The benefit of this corporate effort to the community is that the Body of Christ becomes recognizable, more whole, and therefore more relevant and more accessible to the community. The benefit of this community effort to the individual churches and ministries is that the House of Prayer becomes a resource to everyone involved.

As individual ministries become involved in their area House of Prayer, their worship teams get more experience under different conditions, sharpening their skills and increasing their exposure. It therefore becomes possible and feasible to raise up multiple worship teams that all may follow their talents and giftings, becoming more experienced and skillful. Through the House of Prayer many groups can begin to share worship resources. In the area of worship, the House of Prayer becomes a training ground, and fertile soil for all kinds of creative expression to spring up – which then flows back into individual churches and ministries, supporting more experienced, more vibrant, more effective worship ministries.

The House of Prayer becomes a major source of prayer support for local ministries, unknown and undreamed of by individual churches and ministries until now. In communities that support a local House of Prayer, many ministries report increased effectiveness, increased blessing on home and church life, and a decrease in the kind of trouble attributable to spiritual warfare. With increased prayer covering through the House of Prayer, churches are reaching goals that

---

[1] The pattern being, of course, in II Chron. 7:14.

were just out of reach when they stood alone.

The local House of Prayer becomes an equipping center for teaching and training in the areas of worship, prayer, intercession, revelation, creative outreach, leadership, and practical ministry. This becomes much more valuable to local churches involved than even a prestigious seminary might be, as individuals flow out of the House of Prayer and into local ministries activated in their talents and giftings. Worshippers lift up the Name of our God with new fervor and heart. Armies of prayer warriors find their voices in prayer and take it into their churches and out into the streets. Intercessors begin to understand their calling, and partner to pray for pastors and leaders. Teachers find the word aflame with new power and meaning. Young leaders begin to practice their giftings in the House of Prayer, and are hungry to come alongside established ministries. Masses of believers hone their skills in practical ministry and want to serve their churches and the poor and needy.

The House of Prayer and John 17

The Church has never been able to make meaningful strides toward one of its most important goals: unity. The kind of unity that Jesus prayed for us before His death is an important and elusive prerequisite to His return. In this area, the House of Prayer clearly shows itself as a key strategic piece of God's end-time plan. The House of Prayer becomes a center available for the building of unity in the Body of Christ, but even more it becomes a group project, a common cause with common goals that draw together diverse segments of the Body. It becomes a place where small differences can be laid aside while we focus on the foundation stones of our faith: worship, prayer, and revelation in the word and from the Spirit of God[1] . It is a place where a diversity of expression is encouraged; silent sessions can compliment expressive sessions, traditionally oriented sessions stand beautifully and meaningfully alongside contemporary youth oriented sessions. The House of Prayer is a place where the simplicity of praying the word can give way to joyful, exuberant arts

---

[1] This whole section is a fulfillment of Col.3:11-14.

expressions. Through the mediating effects inherent within the purposes and goals of the House of Prayer the local Body of Christ comes together for the building of unity toward a goal: the vibrancy and effectiveness of the City-wide or regional Church.

A Resource to the community at large

In addition to being a resource to local churches and ministries, the House of Prayer becomes a resource to the community at large. As a community expression of the Body of Christ in an area, the House of Prayer becomes an open door to people who may never visit a church building. The pursuit and expression of our worship and prayer through the arts becomes an intriguing venue. Arts expression spawns arts groups and instruction, which will be an attractive draw for many who would never have come into contact with more specific church-related activities. Just the active presence of this kind of multi-media format of worship and prayer will be a draw and an outreach to our increasingly media-oriented culture. The format will be an attraction, and the open content of worship, prayer and revelation will be a powerful vehicle to draw people into the presence of God. We've seen that from there it is just a small step into the Kingdom.

Further, as the Body of Christ in an area begins to grasp God's heart for their community in prayer, the House of Prayer becomes a base for community development. The heart abandoned to God begins to beat with His love for the lost. This dynamic of the House of Prayer eventually turns it into a staging area to meet the needs of the community with the love of Christ. Feeding the hungry, visiting the lonely and healing the sick become areas of ministry within the House of Prayer that begins to draw members of the community through its doors. Once inside, friendly faces, a loving word, an experience in the presence of God is all that is needed for many to come to the loving embrace of Jesus.

One of the practical ministries of love that is increasingly becoming a part of the House of Prayer is the ministry of healing rooms. As the heart of Jesus for the sick, lost and broken is manifested in the hearts of people through the experience of the House of Prayer, it becomes a natural thing to open a space for the ministry of healing prayer. The results of such a ministry can be amazing, as simple Christians take up a heart to pray for the sick. The heart of Jesus is tangibly manifested, and the power of the Holy Spirit is released for healing. As people are healed, the community will begin to come in.

A big part of the purpose of the House of Prayer is investing in the city through prayer. This kind of sustained, focused prayer goes a long way in bringing about changes in a community. In addition, such a prayer effort cultivates a heart for the community in the people of God. This will eventually and quite naturally begin to flow out in practical expressions of the heart of Jesus for the city or region[1]. Individuals will begin to reach out with the love of Christ as they go about their daily business. Groups will begin to meet in public gathering places to pray, strike up conversations, and begin to minister God's love to people's felt needs. Soon the investment of prayer for the city from within the House of Prayer finds a natural yet dynamic outlet as this investment flows out into the streets through expressions of practical outreach[2]. This sets the stage for the kind of community transformation that we have dreamed of and prayed for in isolation for years[3].

A Resource to the world

As the House of Prayer matures it develops a "repertoire" of worship and arts expressions as these expressions are woven into worship and prayer in sessions every day. These expressions mature as the artists advance in experience and skill in the House of Prayer. In time these high-quality arts expressions begin to flow out into the local arts and media venues. Musicians from the House of Prayer bring their songs to local cafes, music festivals and make them available in recordings. Painters who pursue their work as worship and intercession within the House of Prayer begin to place their paintings

---

[1] We will "do good to all people", Gal. 6:10.
[2] Luke 14:23.
[3] As in Psalm 126:1-3. As a promise of the restoration of Zion, this whole chapter is a promise to those of us working to establish the House of Prayer.

in local galleries, as they become known through arts fairs and showings. Writers and poets in the House of Prayer begin to publish their work; dancers to perform in local shows; video and film artists begin to show at film festivals.

Much of this work is initially developed and used in the House of Prayer, and carries a depth of meaning and spiritual anointing that makes these expressions tools of outreach to the community and to the world wherever they are shown, performed or exhibited. This phenomenon associated with the work of the House of Prayer has been seen here and there in communities where the House of Prayer has become established – it will be a much larger force in the world of arts and media as the House of Prayer grows, spreads, and matures in cities around the globe. The world will be increasingly touched by the growing force of the House of Prayer as the transformed life of the Body of Christ begins flowing out in living evangelistic power through individuals, through community efforts and through creative media forged in the fires of worship, intercession and revelation.

As God's heart for the community flows forth, the heart of God for Mercy and Justice for the nations begins to rise up within the House of Prayer. The House of Prayer develops a functional aspect of missions ministry base with the cultivation of circles of local and international mercy ministries. Mercy ministries that have sprung up and are currently functioning around Houses of Prayer embody a heart for Children at Risk, for widows and orphans[1], for brotherhood with and the salvation of Israel[2], for the hungry and destitute[3] and for those suffering from wars and disasters around the world[4]. In cultivating a heart for the lost and needy on a local level, the House of Prayer serves as a nucleus, as a support structure, and as a home base for many mercy ministries to spring up that reach out with the Love of Christ to people around the world.

---

[1] Strongly established in the Old Testament, as well as the new. See James 1:27.
[2] Strongly supported in the word, yet much misunderstood. See Rom. 10:1; & 11:14.
[3] Psalm 41:1.
[5] Is. 58:7.

Conclusion

As a work of priestly teams planting in the earth the different functions of heaven, the House of Prayer becomes a work that must draw on, and draw together the different characteristics of the whole Body of Christ in a region. The House of Prayer must be an effort of the whole Body of Christ. There are deep spiritual reasons that the work of the House of Prayer must be the work of the Body at large in a city or area.

The House of Prayer is a key part of the fulfillment of the prayer of Jesus for unity within the Body of Christ in Matthew chapter seventeen.

As the House of Prayer begins to function as a work of the whole body, it begins to function as a valuable resource to local churches and ministries, and a much needed resource to the body of Christ at large.

As these roles of unity and resource for the people of God grow and begin to bear fruit, the House of Prayer becomes a source of truth and life that flows out of the confines of the church and to the people in a city or area.

…and out into the world!

CH 10 The House of Prayer and Kingdom Enterprise

God has given us a concept of Kingdom enterprise that we call Tentmakers. We see the House of Prayer as a hub connecting and supporting local churches and outreach ministries, surrounded by Kingdom enterprises. The House of Prayer pours into the local Body and Kingdom Business with prayer, equipping, and experienced practical ministry teams, while the local ministries and Kingdom enterprises respond with a reciprocal flow back into the House of Prayer with hearts, hands and resources.

Tentmakers specifically is a small business support network that is dedicated to furthering of the kingdom of God in the earth. Within that overarching goal we help to develop small business enterprises that will use profits to strengthen Christian families and communities, and also promote the work of the Kingdom in the House of Prayer.

The concept of business that we are developing in both the formation and transaction of business in our world today is described as Kingdom Business. The term Kingdom Business is not a description of a business that is merely owned or run by Christians. This is only a minute part of the overall concept. What we are describing is a reality where every aspect of the operation of a business is seen as an extension of the Kingdom of God.

What makes a Kingdom Business is the position from which it is approached, transacted or executed, the Kingdom community needs the business fulfills, and what uses profits are put to. That position is shaped by a level of understanding and insight into God's plan to further His purposes in the local community, and infiltrate the marketplace and the local community with His kingdom power and values.

We see business as part of the life of the Kingdom, and as part of the global plan of God. Kingdom Businesses can become strategic tools through which God will fulfill His promises: of prosperity for His people, for the rebuilding of the ancient foundations of the House of Prayer and Worship in the earth, and of transferring the wealth of the nations to the purposes of the Kingdom of God[1]. Kingdom Businesses can also be strategic and tactical implements for confronting the heart of selfishness within the world of commerce, tools for making the kingdoms of this world into the kingdoms of our God.

Tentmakers is committed to:
- Pursuing small business and micro enterprise that can support Christian families, communities, ministers and missionaries.
- Encouraging the development of small business and micro enterprise that will follow the Kingdom Business model.
- Assisting in creating business entities that function as platforms for Kingdom values, Kingdom life, and Kingdom power in the earth.
- Supporting Kingdom ministry, especially the local House of Prayer and Worship, community outreach, and global missions.

Principles for Kingdom Business

As I began to teach what the Lord had been speaking to me concerning the vision of the House of Prayer, in particular in its partnership with Kingdom Business, a woman approached me after a class who was visibly affected. She described her own vision for the House of Prayer, and briefly related a vision for community that her husband was carrying. She told me that she was beginning to see, in the intersection between The House of Prayer and Kingdom Business, that her and her husband's visions were one and the same. She told me that her husband had written some papers on community and business

---

[1] This dynamic can be seen in Prov. 13:22, as well as many other scriptures.

in the Kingdom of God, and asked if I would like to read them. I mentioned that I was looking for reviewers for the earliest drafts of this book, and I would be glad to share on each side. For a number of weeks coming and going from classes she curried manuscripts and messages between her husband and me in a growing and mutual admiration.

I did not know, of course, that God was setting me up. This man that I had never met began emailing to me the best feedback I had yet gotten on my book, while I read and enjoyed His writing as well. At one point I began to realize that some of his writing needed to be incorporated in this chapter. After all, he wrote like he had the experience in the business world that I lacked. Where my perspective on Kingdom Business was theoretical, his was founded in the wisdom of extensive practice. I asked if the two of us could meet to discuss our writing in more depth.

When we met I was overwhelmed to recognize that I had been corresponding with a well known and respected corporate leader in the community. This is a man who I normally would have been too intimidated to cultivate any meaningful relationship with. This man was Michael Mooney, businessman and corporate architect who works with substantial companies and churches, as well as developing his own.

Since the time of our meeting Michael has become a friend and mentor in my life, patiently helping to chart the course of my dynamic and often eruptive visionary nature. Before long we were collaborating on many projects together, including the rest of this chapter. Enough of the theoretical discussion, let's get to some of the wisdom of Michael's experience.

An Illustration From the Body

The heart of a human body will die unless it is sustained by other members. The mind must seek out "bread and water" – the basics of life for the maintenance of the body. I know you enjoy more than "bread and water" – I too enjoy a latte! But I think you know what I mean.

The hand must lift the "bread and water" to the mouth for ingestion. The stomach must convert the bread and water to usable energy and life providing products for the body. These essential products are then forwarded to the heart which then forwards the "life that is in the blood" back to the rest of the body. So it is with the House of Prayer and Kingdom Business.

Spiritually speaking, the House of Prayer represents the heart. It travails. Its members cause a flow of living waters out of the heart of heaven through prayer and intercession. It listens to the heart throb of Him who is seated at the right hand of the Father, and it listens to the groaning of the Spirit. The House of Prayer taps into the sound of the heavenly metronome as the times of visitation are in the Father's heart. But the heart – in its hidden and vital function buried in the chest – is heavily dependent on all of the body's members. Without that interdependent and symbiotic relation, the heart will die. And when the heart dies, the body dies. Is it any wonder that the church is in its current anemic state?

Kingdom Business represents members of the Body of Christ responsible for bringing resources for life on earth (bread and water) to the heart. This living, corporate picture of interdependence is a macrocosm of family life where the "bread-winner" provides for the family's life and existence.

There is a holy honor in bread winning to provide for Christ's body, one's family and God's community on earth. This function is not "second class" to the heart nor is it superior to the heart. God has so constituted the body that each member has need of one another. This analogy is not to suggest that only the formal members of the House of Prayer pray. God forbid! Members gifted of the Father for ministry in Kingdom Business should also pray and co-labor with the House of Prayer. Does not each member of the body – even to the smallest cell – have an intimate connection with the flow of blood from the heart? But it is the work of the heart to get that necessary flow out to the body at large.

This analogy is not to suggest that only the formal members of Kingdom Business work. God forbid! Did not Jesus and Paul labor in their respective areas to help provide for those with them? Did not

Jesus say that He was about His Father's work as he preached and prayed?

So whether on our knees, hands raised in worship, cleaning latrines, setting up shop, or sitting in a board room with other negotiators, we all are called to work diligently and interdependently in order to make this Kingdom work. All of these things are honorable, provided the work we do is centered in His rest. In contemporary terms of what is in vogue in the Spirit, "striving is out; rest is in".

God's Body-based Model

How then is a new, cooperative, body-based model actualized in our 20th century work world? What principles are eternal and inviolate? What is culturally permissible and appropriate? Let's begin with what we know. After all, there are some familiar foundations we can stand on as we explore this concept.

As **business men and women**, we are already aware of the division of revenue and expenses in a corporation. There are those responsible for making money – we call them the "Marketing and Sales" departments. There are those responsible for spending money – research and development, personnel, plant and equipment -- there seem to be many of those departments! Some wise, some unwise.

In **government** we see this division of revenue and expenses as well. We see the work of "rendering unto Caesar" to support governments and programs. We see the work of Caesar's expenditures – roadways and infrastructure, social services, bookkeeping and analysis. Some wise, some unwise.

In **families** we see this division of revenue and expense. We see the breadwinners at work -- some traditional, others less so. We see the expense side at work in our housing and utility costs, grocery budget, or the monthly AMEX or Visa bill. Some wise, some unwise. In **churches** we also see this division of revenue and expense. We see the revenue provision in the offerings. We see the expense side in staff, buildings and works of ministry. Some wise, some unwise, on and on it goes. The heavenly ways are modeled - unknowingly and at least in part - by many.

The call and burden of the Holy Spirit in our day is to create foundations and practices that not only reflect God's Kingdom processes and structures, but institute and integrate them firmly into our daily life activities. Let's re-state that with an emphasis on the topic at hand: The call and burden of the Holy Spirit in our day is to create business foundations and practices that not only reflect God's economic processes and structures, but institute them firmly in our ways and means of doing business. There is no more excuse for business as usual!

But there is the rub! Forces of old are marshaled against this holy transition to God's Kingdom ways. Was not the strength of the enemy in the form of the King of Tyre of a master merchant? Was not Pharaoh in Egypt particularly stubborn about letting go of what he considered his economic resources, namely the children of Israel enslaved under the whip?

It was only through holy intercession – through Moses stretching forth his staff in the power of the Father's mighty hand – that freedom and the riches of Egypt were released to God's chosen people. Let us not, then, underestimate the task. Putting our hand into God's hand and walking forward with our eyes open to the schemes of our enemy is the only way to start, and we accomplish both of these in intimacy with God, with much strategic prayer and intercession. Only a fool goes to war without counting the cost. Even modern generals like Norman Schwarzkopf in Desert Storm know to measure the enemy's capabilities well before implementing a plan.

Kingdom Businesses are businesses led and controlled by a person or persons who are committed to making their business a part of the present day purposes of God. Building out Kingdom Business, however, requires the implementation of key principles and values. We will now set some of these forth for your prayerful consideration. Bear with me while I speak "straight up" with you on some key areas. From there, we will then sum up with a definition of what it means to be a Kingdom Business. Such businesses will manifest many of the following characteristics:

Ten Principles of Kingdom Business

Principle # 1 – *Ongoing effectual, fervent prayer is absolutely essential.*

Do not (I repeat, **DO NOT**) attempt to grow a Kingdom Business without the heart of prayer behind you. You are no match – without divine wisdom and enabling – for the prince of darkness. Remember the king of Tyre? The enemy knows more about business than you might imagine. It is necessary for emerging Kingdom Business to team with intercessors within Houses of Prayer. The first key to Kingdom Business is to build everything upon a strong structure of prayer.

Principle # 2 – *Your business work has value in fulfilling prophetic promises.*

Oh, so you are just a workman toiling in business when the real spiritual stuff is in the "ministry", or in the House of Prayer with the priests? Who told you **that** one? Maybe, just maybe, your success in Kingdom Business will save the souls of many! Kingdom Businesses must see themselves as significant components for the implementation of prophetic promises for apostolic times (times to strategically implement biblical patterns). They are real implements of the work of the Kingdom of God, and not separate entities in themselves. Your business work is an integral part of Kingdom ministry in the earth!

Principle # 3 – *You must die.*

Ouch! The mighty Apostle Paul reported that he died daily. Jesus – the Lamb of God – was slain before the foundation of this world. The servant is not above his Master. Your Achilles' heel is your view of your ability to generate money. Your strength is His granted abilities and grace to acquire wealth. Do you see the difference? Both look almost the same on the surface. One comes from our own strength, and will be hijacked by the enemy of our souls. The other comes from heaven, and relies on God alone. You can only get to the heavenly through the personal cross and a personal resurrection. Biblical character is of vital and central importance! Every aspect of the operation of any Kingdom Business must be founded, built and regulated upon the principles of biblical character and God's Kingdom economy. If this "death thing" makes no *real* sense to you at this point in your life, I encourage you to ask the Father to make it real and bring you into this central truth.

Principle # 4 – *You must walk in relationship with the local assembly of saints God has called you to.*

Yes, we all know there is dysfunction within the Church. Jesus came to save sinners, and we all have fallen short. Money is not a shortcut to sainthood. Aspiring to become a power-broker on the board of deacons is a shortcut to a spirit of control that will shipwreck Kingdom Business. Real people with real struggles pushing buttons and developing longsuffering inside you is what will really grow you up. Suffer with His people – that was Moses' choice too. There is a perspective for Kingdom Business that can only come through the Community of His people. Warts and all. Kingdom Businesses must build strong relationship networks within and among local churches and ministries, and must operate cooperatively in the covenant of love and commitment with the members of the Body of Christ -- not in manipulation and control. This places a requirement upon both Kingdom Business and the local body for mature, relational teambuilding and "submission one to another".

Principle # 5 – *The Holy Spirit likes to negotiate and do business*!

While the enemy of our souls is well-studied in business, he is no match for the Author of Business. Kingdom Business relies on revelation, wisdom, words of knowledge, discernment and prophetic insight. These gifts can give us an edge, giving Kingdom advantage in creative ideas, foresight of trends and new developments; in negotiation, contracts, interaction with people; with difficult decisions, and much more. When Kingdom Business teams live and move in the consciousness of the light of the presence of God, we will be supernaturally activated to establish the Kingdom through our business efforts. These supernatural activation points are not "church gifts" or gifts available only inside of a church building. They are the tools of Kingdom builders given to establish God's Kingdom in the earth. Skip these tools and you will play into the hands of Satan. Embrace these gifts as tools through your personal cross, inter-dependence with His Body and a genuine love for the saints and the lost, and you will see Kingdom miracles!

Principle # 6 – *Submit to the Holy Spirit's renewing of your mind.*

I remain amazed at how often spiritual principles are not applied to the realm of business. We study the application of spiritual principles within marriage, inter-personal relationships and within our church life. And yet, we somehow seem to only bring a fraction of this thought-life and approach into the realm of business. Ask the Lord how to bring every thought captive to His approach to business. Do not lean or depend on the shadow of Egypt – even if that treasured thought or principle came from your favorite business school professor or your trusted business mentor. Kingdom Businesses must be vitally plugged into the larger apostolic paradigm – a paradigm of planting and establishing the works of the Kingdom of God in the earth, that the "Kingdoms of this world will become the Kingdom of Our LORD, and of His Christ". Every aspect of a business – its culture, its bookkeeping, its customer service, its commitment to excellence, its relations with personnel -- must reflect this Kingdom mentality in creativity, discipline, faith, breakthrough, prosperity[1], success, global mentality, team leadership and networking. The World says, "If I give from what I have I will have less; the Word says, "If we give, more shall be given to us[2]."

Principle # 7 – *Position yourself to receive apostolic exhortation.*

---

[1] If we believe the Word of God and implement it, we will prosper: Josh. 1:8; II Chr. 20:20.
[2] Jesus said it in Luke 6:38.

Apostles and leaders within the Body of Christ are given of God as vessels to equip and serve the saints. Kingdom Businesses must be relationally linked to groups and ministers who can give counsel, guidance, and impartation of grace, favor and energy. The culture of the business must reflect apostolic trends such as creativity, discipline, faith, breakthrough, prosperity, success, a global mentality and networking. People are drawn to creativity!

Principle # 8 – *Get involved and network.*

Consider the life of Nehemiah, Isaiah or Cyrus. Do they strike you as being in the holy huddle of "Christian Business" like little islands away from the rest of mankind? Not a chance! Let your light shine! You are an open door for people to come to for the Commerce of the Spirit. Kingdom Businesses must embrace a vision of themselves as contact points for the Body of Christ to the world's centers of influence in economics, commerce, and politics. Every Kingdom Business becomes a new entrance point for God's Kingdom to invade the commercial systems of the world – whether on Main Street or on Wall Street.

Jeremiah 51:31-33 can be seen as a picture of what God is doing in our day in the area of Kingdom Business: "…messenger by messenger…" Kingdom Businesses are networking within commercial systems to build a global Kingdom net of economic influence, thereby serving the enemy notice of the end of His world economic rule. These business entities must be very clean of the world's ways, and have minimum reliance on world economic structures so that when the systems fall they will not be broken. In Revelation 18 it is the apostles and prophets who rejoice when Babylon is shattered[1]. These apostles and prophets can be seen as a general indication of the apostolic networks of the Kingdom of God in the earth[2], separated from yet actively countering that which is corrupt. Whether it is in economics,

---

[1] Rev. 18:20.
[2] Eph. 2:19,20.

commerce, or through appropriate political influence, you are being called to make a difference!

Principle #9 – *Have kids.*

I'm not talking about the offspring of your family union. I'm talking about the hard-at-times road of learning the ropes of Kingdom Business and then sharing the journey and principles with others. Kingdom Businesses must have the mentality of reproducers. They must walk in the kingdom principles of fathering and mentoring. The Kingdom paradigm is so far distant from the concepts of grasping and competition that pervade the mindset of the world and its systems. God's Kingdom paradigm calls us to be fruitful and multiply[1]: helping to birth new Kingdom Businesses and fathering those new and emerging businesses into activation in their Kingdom destiny[2]. Many are looking for answers and pathways in the spirit. You can be a lighthouse to help guide other ships of Kingdom commerce. You must be a father to the next generation in Kingdom Business.

Principle #10 – *Give.*

Take a hard look at what you really need. God isn't against wealth, and sometimes will gift people with things that seem *considerably* above the subsistence level. This is usually a function of the level to which individuals are called to reach out with the truth of the Kingdom into the upper echelons of the world. It was right that Solomon did not live like a pauper -- he was called to bring the truth to many of the ancient world's elite. However God calls us to live, whether we are abased or abound, we must keep our focus on the one who has called us, and His greater purposes. One of the central callings of Kingdom Business is as a provisioning arm of the advance of the Kingdom of God in the earth. Resourcing the Kingdom under the direction of the Holy Spirit must be a major purpose and goal of

---

[1] Gen. 1:27, 28.
[2] Just as Paul expressed in Gal. 4:19.

any Kingdom Business. To achieve this goal there must be a deliberate, systematic, structural commitment to regularly give of business resources to Kingdom works. Team up with the House of Prayer to help meet their needs. Work with them to be corridors of giving to others. Freely you have received, freely give!

To Sum Up

In conclusion I would like to share with you my own definition of what it means to be a Kingdom Business. As a Kingdom Business we want to:

"PARTNER WITH HIS PRAYING PRIESTS TO CONTEND WITH THE WORLD'S FORCES, ACQUIRE WEALTH LAWFULLY THROUGH THE SPIRIT, AND RESOURCE GOD'S WORK IN THE EARTH".

As contenders for the faith, **we must learn how to fight**. God is a man of war (Exodus 15). You will need the 10 principles above to fight the good fight and build out a Kingdom Business. Your weapons are mighty in God to pull down strongholds. This is where teaming up with a House of Prayer provides a significant business advantage to you. A word of warning: Do not pursue Kingdom Business just for some kind of personal or financial advantage. If you are looking for personal advantage it is much more "reasonable" and "safe" to stay yoked to the world and its systems. Do it for an advantage and it will turn into a curse. If, however, you are dedicated to the advance of the Kingdom of God, and you want to position your business and business life to provision that advance bringing the light of God's presence into the darkness of the world, GO FOR IT! Do it with the right heart, and all of heaven will be at your side! Welcome to Moses' court. Welcome to the Heavenly War Room. May His blessings rest upon you as you take the promised land of Kingdom Commerce!

CH 11 David's Heart for The Temple, and The Establishment Of The House of Prayer Today

"Then David said, 'The house of the LORD God is to be here, and also the altar of burnt offering for Israel'" I Chronicles 22:1.

In I Chronicles 21-26 we see a parallel between David's desire to establish the House of The LORD in His time and God's desire to establish The House of Prayer today. We can see in this passage a type of God the Father in David the king. We can also see a type of us, the sons of God on the earth, in Solomon (shalom-on, or "man of peace", "Blessed are the peacemakers, for they shall inherit the earth...") the son of David.

Jesus is our king, and as you may remember, David paid the full price for the redemption of his people from plague. He set up an altar on the threshing floor of Araunah (Ark), insisted on paying the full price, and made a sacrifice. The plague was stopped (I Chron. 21). Jesus is our redeemer who has paid the full price for our sins[1]. He is our ark in which we can find safety, healing and redemption from the plague of sin and death. He has made the ultimate sacrifice for our redemption, and the plague of sin and death over us is broken! The angel of separation from God that has guarded the garden of fellowship with God through the centuries has "put his sword back into its sheath"[2] because of the sacrifice of Christ! The way into that dear fellowship has been opened to us in Christ[3].

---

[1] Jesus said "it is finished!" ie: complete -- John 19:30.
[2] The angel referred to is found in I Chron. 21:27; Jesus has, however, "put away" sin and its consequences by the sacrifice of himself – Heb. 9:26.
[3] I Jn. 1:3b, now "...our fellowship is with the Father, and with His son, Jesus

In this day we feel the heart of God calling to our hearts[1] to establish houses of prayer and worship. In this day God is calling us to establish altars instead of thrones, because the time of the casting down of thrones is upon us.

We have heard the heart of God speaking in just the same way David did when he said: "The house of the LORD God is to be here, and also the altar of burnt offering for Israel." Where is here? David is speaking of the threshing floor of Araunah, the place of the altar of sacrifice. In the same way, God is pronouncing that we begin to build a house for His Name in the place of Christ's sacrifice, the place where we follow Christ into His sacrifice, the threshing floor in our lives where God has led us to follow into Christ's death. Many of us have been obedient to follow God's directions down into darkness, death and obscurity. We have been threshed in a big way. But this is a place of safety. If we follow in obedience down into death with Christ, if we are obedient to this suffering, God promises complete and glorious resurrection[2]! This may now be our threshing floor, but this is soon to be the place where the ark of His presence will be established!

So God says that this place, this place of threshing and sacrifice is the place of our ark... the place where we are to build the glorious place of His presence – the House of Prayer, the House of the LORD established in the earth!

> "*2 So David gave orders to assemble the aliens living in Israel, and from among them he appointed stonecutters to prepare dressed stone for building the house of God.*"

In this day God has given orders to angelic hosts, appointing stonecutters to prepare living stones for the building of the house of God[3]. Our hearts are stirred; we've had a taste of His presence in this new move and we have to have more[4]. Our hearts are hungry to see

---

Christ..."
[1] Ps. 42:7, deep is calling out to deep!
[2] Rom. 6:5,8.
[3] I Pet. 2:5.
[4] We have "tasted" the good word of God and the powers of the world to come –

the House of Prayer and Worship established. He's preparing us to establish it! He is preparing our hearts as living stones for the building of His house.

> "*⁵ David said, 'My son Solomon is young and inexperienced, and the house to be built for the LORD should be of great magnificence and fame and splendor in the sight of all the nations. Therefore I will make preparations for it.' So David made extensive preparations...*"

Our Father God is so good to us. He knows we are made of dust[1]. He knows that we are young and inexperienced in spiritual things. He knows that the job He is calling us to is well beyond our capabilities. We have a vision of the House of Prayer, and it is to be GREAT in the earth! The vision that we are carrying for the establishment of The house of the LORD is magnificent and splendid beyond our means or capacity to build it. But God wants us to know that He has made extensive preparations for the establishment of His house at this time, before we even were brought into the project[2].

> "*⁶ Then he called for his son Solomon and charged him to build a house for the LORD, the God of Israel. ⁷ David said to Solomon: "My son, I had it in my heart to build a house for the Name of the LORD my God. ⁸ But this word of the LORD came to me: 'You have shed much blood and have fought many wars. You are not to build a house for my Name, because you have shed much blood on the earth in my sight. ⁹ But you will have a son who will be a man of peace and rest, and I will give him rest from all his enemies on every side. His name will be Solomon and I will grant Israel peace and quiet during his reign. ¹⁰ He is the one who will build a house for my Name. He will be my son, and I will be his father. And I will establish the throne of his kingdom over Israel forever.'"*

Heb. 6:5, and we have "tasted" and seen that the Lord is gracious – I Pet. 2:3.
[1] Ps. 103:14.
[2] Is. 42:9.

Christ could have done it all. Christ could have done it all without even dying. Jesus could have come, established His kingdom, and reigned eternally without any problem. HE IS THE SOVEREIGN OF THE UNIVERSE! But God Himself submitted to death for the joy set before Him[1]. And what was that joy? The joy that was set before Him was us! Christ died to bring us into sonship, into bridehood; Christ laid His life down to save us, to redeem us, to bring us into our inheritance as heirs and joint heirs with Himself[2], as the Bride of Christ! In this passage God is prophesying that He will have for Himself a son, a man of peace heir to Christ Himself.

This is the son, the people whom the Spirit of God will prepare in the last days of the world to establish a house in the earth whose purpose is to worship and lift up His name, His kingdom, as it is in heaven. This is the work that will hallow the Name of YHWH in the earth and establish the kingdom of heaven on earth! This is the House of Prayer and Worship that the Spirit and our hearts long to establish right now[3]. This is the work that He is establishing among us so that we can begin to make the kingdoms of this world into the kingdoms of Our LORD, and of His Christ[4], and from this house He will progressively reign, until He reigns all forever and ever[5]! Jesus could have done it all himself, but he wanted us! He wanted to establish us in the earth, so that He could establish this house in us, so that He could establish His glory in this house, so that He could have us as His glorious Bride participating in His rulership into eternity. God the Father is commissioning us, charging us to build this house in this day, so that His glorious Name can be established in the earth!

> *"I Chr. 20:11 'Now, my son, the LORD be with you, and may you have success and build the house of the LORD your God, as he said you would. ¹² May the LORD give you discretion*

---

[1] Heb. 12:2.
[2] Rom. 8:17.
[3] Rev. 22:17 – "...the Spirit and the Bride say Come!"
[4] Rev. 11:15.
[5] I Cor. 15:25.

and understanding when he puts you in command over Israel, so that you may keep the law of the LORD your God. ¹³ Then you will have success if you are careful to observe the decrees and laws that the LORD gave Moses for Israel. Be strong and courageous. Do not be afraid or discouraged.'"

God is calling us to build His House of Prayer and Worship in the earth at this time, and He is commanding success and His presence over us. Do not mistake this, for when God commands success, we will have success! When God directly commands His presence like He is now, at this time, we should get ready for His presence in a big way! He goes on, however, and commands discretion and understanding over us so that we will keep His law. Keep the Law??? What does keeping the law have to do with establishing the House of Prayer?

I would say that it has everything to do with it. We are living in the time of the restoration of all things. God is in the midst of restoring many things to the church that we have lost over the ages. God is restoring power to the church. God is restoring the tabernacle of David in our midst. God is also restoring the promises of His covenant, if the church can plug into His purposes throughout history and learn to live by the law of Love[1]. I understand that there is a very real danger in the notion of "keeping the Law" that may seem to fly in the face of Paul's teaching in Galatians, especially if the reader takes this section incorrectly due to emotional reaction, challenging past experiences, poor theology or what have you. Some could misunderstand this point and go merrily about packing a lamb into the House of Prayer and setting up a Pentateuch style altar. This is not what I intend to espouse here – after all, this could get rather messy and we all would need mint sauce. All jesting aside, it is very important that the man of the Spirit "use the law lawfully" to avoid this sort of error.

The truth is that the current excesses in the other direction have lead to a fear of the law, antinomianism and a fundamental disregard for God's heart in giving us His Law. The sacrifice of Jesus is more

---

[1] See Rom. 13:8-10. Paul states here that love is the fulfilling of the law – this is the law of love.

than sufficient, once and for all, so that if we follow our lover and Lord by the Spirit, He will lead us into all truth[1]. Embracing this truth does not mean embracing a list of rules and regulations, but a commanded practice of Love for God first and then for our brothers here on earth[2]. This practice can be cultivated within our hearts in an intimate relationship with Him. This practice of Love comes with an entire library of promises that have been collected for us, to show us that they can all be ours if we will nurture the practice of Love in the secret place with Him.

Embracing the practice of the law of love is not an impossibility. He is commanding over us the discretion and understanding to do it. Jesus died to give us the power to do it. God is now proclaiming over us the strength and the courage to do it. We cannot go any further unless we are willing to begin to do it.

> *"[14] 'I have taken great pains to provide for the temple of the LORD a hundred thousand talents (about 3,750 tons, or about 3,450 metric tons) of gold, a million talents (about 37,500 tons, or about 34,500 metric tons) of silver, quantities of bronze and iron too great to be weighed, and wood and stone. And you may add to them."*

Like David of old, God is excited by His plans to build this new establishment of heaven among us. He is commissioning us as sons, priests and kings to begin the project. What's more, God is pronouncing, in this day, that He has taken great pains to provide everything that we will need to commence the building of His great and glorious house. We merely have to gather the resources that He has provided for this purpose, dedicate our efforts, and begin. He has supplied abundantly, more than we could ask, think or measure. Further, we may add to His supply. He is calling His people to give.

> *[15] "You have many workmen: stonecutters, masons and*

---

[1] John 13:16.
[2] Matt. 22:37-40; Mk. 12:30,31.

> *carpenters, as well as men skilled in every kind of work [16] in gold and silver, bronze and iron-craftsmen beyond number. Now begin the work, and the LORD be with you."*

This movement has hit the earth like a great upwelling flood. There are uncounted hearts that ache to begin to establish the House of Prayer in communities across the globe. There are lives, like my life, and the lives of my family, that are dedicated completely to bringing this establishment of heaven to reality in the earth. In our day God has supplied great provision, and He has equipped the body with many workmen skilled in every kind of work. Many of these workmen that God has equipped for the calling of building the House of Prayer in the earth do not know at this time that this is what they are to do. They may feel a nagging restlessness in their current work. They may feel as if there must be more, something more fulfilling. Many, like myself and others, are beginning or ready to begin. Whatever our current response to the call, we all will begin to hear and respond[1] as the work of the establishment begins to go forward in our cities.

> [17] *"Then David ordered all the leaders of Israel to help his son Solomon. [18] He said to them, "Is not the LORD your God with you? And has he not granted you rest on every side? For he has handed the inhabitants of the land over to me, and the land is subject to the LORD and to his people."*

Some say that the House of Prayer is in each heart. I agree with this statement. Many say that the House of Prayer is a function of the church. This is also true. Others argue that the House of Prayer is primarily a spiritual construct. This is true as well. All of these statements are true, yet as long as they are used to support the status quo and hold back the vision and resources that God is raising up for the physical establishment of Houses of Prayer in the earth, the church will merely go on in its current condition, with little of what God has promised fulfilled.

---

[1] Like young Samuel of old we say "

We are in a time when God is challenging many of us who have ears to hear to put our hands, hearts and resources to work to see the House of Prayer established in our communities[1]. The House of Prayer is a physical establishment of the work of heaven in the earth. As such it is the seed of heaven planted among us. As long as we will not plant the seed, we will not see the fruit. We all long for God's kingdom to come among us in power. We sing and pray for revival to come, but God is revealing to us an important part of His strategy, foretold throughout the scriptures, for establishing His move in the earth: the restoration of David's tabernacle! The House of Prayer is the seed, the kernel of heaven planted in the earth to help prepare His bride, to help equip the body, to contain the power of heaven so that it may begin to flow forth into the world.

There are some already walking in this place. The Psalmist talks about "Thy Hidden Ones". The House of Prayer, however, will create a catalyst for a much broader and pervasive actualization of this work of the Spirit and His Kingdom on earth.

Once the House of Prayer is established and in operation in a community, then many more Christians will learn to walk in the work of heaven[2], and their hearts will be Houses of Prayer. At that point the churches will have begun to learn to walk in love[3], and they will be Houses of Prayer. Then the Bride will be prepared in the earth, and her heart will function as the spiritual House of Prayer all over the world.

The purpose, then, of the establishment of the physical House of Prayer is to be an establishment of worship, intercession and revelation in the earth so that everyone who will can come and learn how to move in the work and the power of heaven. The purpose of the physical House of Prayer is to offer a neutral connecting point for the

---

[1] Neh. 4:6. When the temple and wall were being rebuilt, the people had "a mind to work" to see it established in spite of the opposition of Sanballat, Tobiah, the Arabs, the Ammonites and the Asdodites. When the people prayed, pulled together their resources, and proceeded to build, the plans of their enemies were frustrated and the wall was built! So it will be with the House of Prayer being established today in spite of opposition.
[2] Judges 7 -- Just like the Israelites after the "faithful 300" won the battle.
[3] Eph. 5:2.

scattered and divided body of Christ that we may come together in unity around the work of heaven and learn to live and move in the power of love. The purpose for establishing the House of Prayer is to open the doors of heaven to the saved and the unsaved alike, 24-hours a day – that all may come all the way into the presence of Almighty God. The purpose of the House of Prayer is to be a center for Kingdom community that forms a platform for the outpouring of the Spirit of God upon all flesh[1], that God's Kingdom would come and His will would be done on the earth in the same way that it is done in heaven[2]. We must devote our hearts, hands and the resources God has given to this call, and begin to establish it!

> *"Now devote your heart and soul to seeking the LORD your God. Begin to build the sanctuary of the LORD God, so that you may bring the ark of the covenant of the LORD and the sacred articles belonging to God into the temple that will be built for the Name of the LORD "*   *I Chronicles 22:19.*

---

[1] Joel 2:28; Acts 2:17.
[2] According to Matt. 6:10.

Section IV - Our Story

CH 12 Dark Days

2009 -- Dark Days in Prayer

The whole country was as hot as a steam room. I was standing in an apartment that had been lent to us, looking out over our new city in Korea. I couldn't see much; it had been pouring down rain on the other side of this plate glass window in front of me for a week. It didn't matter that I couldn't see through the torrential rain. I stood there crying out through tears as I poured my heart out to God. I was all alone.

My family was visiting loved ones in California. I had been with them, but felt disconnected. A dark cloud hovered over me as I tried to enjoy the California sunshine. After a couple weeks I came back to Korea to look for work. We had just moved our things into the borrowed apartment and the air conditioning hadn't been connected yet. It had been over 100 degrees and 100 percent humidity for days now, with the steaming July monsoon rains pouring down. The streets of the city were flooded, there was news of landslides and the ubiquitous Korean black mold was beginning to break out in swaths on the walls, the furniture and the moving boxes piled up around me. I was stalwart; crying out to God in front of my borrowed plate glass window.

This book, as you have read it up to now, was written from unfolding revelation I received as my family and I were working as leadership in The War Room House of Prayer and the House of Prayer Training School in Kelowna, British Columbia, Canada. It holds the core revelation behind everything that we do, and is the central text in the training school. Yet for years people who read this book were disappointed that it had no ending! The book had no ending because it related the revelation for God's calling on the rest of our lives -- and when it was published we hadn't lived any more of it out yet! This chapter and the next tell the story of the first steps of the establishment of the Ring of Fire Houses of Prayer as we have moved forward carrying this immense vision.

    By the time I was standing in front of the plate glass window in Korea we had been carrying the vision of the House of Prayer for over ten years. We had sung it, preached it, taught it, led it, prophesied it, proclaimed it, and continually cried out to God for it. We had implemented the vision of the House of Prayer in our church in California and seen a local move of God. We answered the call to help establish The War Room and the House of Prayer Training School in Kelowna. We had followed God to Korea and established a Christian school, worship communities and the K-1 House of Prayer in Seoul. We worked and prayed. We didn't stop. We nurtured others… we taught worship, prayer and revelation… we challenged everyone who would listen. We had walked it out as far as we could in the U.S., Canada and Korea.

    I was now at my lowest point to date. I couldn't believe that after ten years of faithful effort we had nothing to show for it. The church back home had failed. The house of prayer in Canada had closed. We had built a Christian school here in Korea, then had been unjustly accused and kicked out. The worship communities were all but closed down now. What was it all for? Where were the houses of prayer established like points of light around the Pacific Rim? Where was the success of God's plan? Where were God's promises? I wept in front of that plate glass window like I had never wept before. I cried out in the pain and anguish of desolation. I wasn't in doubt; I knew God's word. I wasn't questioning God -- I knew His promises were true. But why had the promises of God led me to this apparent dead end?

2010 -- The Vision Springing Up in Prayer

During the ensuing year God gave us new jobs, a new apartment, new friends and new avenues for ministry. Yet a year later I was still standing and praying in front of the window in my living room. This time God had plunged me into a time of fasting and prayer. Every day I was calling out for the nations around the Pacific Rim. I would pray over the map of the world, laying my hands on it and calling out the nations by name. I collected maps of all these nations, praying over them, calling out the names of regions and cities. I was drawn to certain areas of Thailand. I was drawn to Northern Myanmar. I especially cried out for Cambodia and Viet Nam. The Philippines was the subject of a major word from an international minister we met. Malaysia and Indonesia are peculiar in that when I pray for them I end up praying for the cities and islands instead of the amalgamated nations. Therefore Singapore, Kuala Lumpur, Sumatra, Java, Borneo, Sulawesi, Bali and New Guinea were prayer and research destinations that year. I read the histories of all these nations and began collecting the accounts of the first missionaries. I prayed especially for Fiji -- God told me not to call the highest mountain in Fiji Mount Victoria, He told me to pray for it using the name Tomanivi. How could I know that this is the name of the mountain in the Fijian native language? I prayed over the Kamchatka Peninsula... over Japan... over the Kurile Islands. I prayed especially over Chile... Ecuador... Costa Rica and the rest of Central America. I prayed for Baja California and the Popocatépetl area in Mexico.

As I prayed, God showed me visions: a house of prayer center nestled at the foot of glacial volcanoes next to an icy sea... deep blue ocean waters bordering a forbidding desert with a house of prayer center backed by snow-capped volcanoes. I saw a center sitting on an inlet opposite majestic volcanic mountains amongst lush jungle next to a tropical sea. This one turned out to be a spot near Khao Sam Roi Yot National Park in Thailand. In another vision I saw a white clapboard village on the ocean. It was a house of prayer center with small businesses, accommodations and an outreach center. I knew that place. It turned out to be Stewarts Point in Sonoma County, my home area. I saw centers in precipitous mountains, on exotic beaches, in luxuriant jungles.

During this time as I prayed, I saw a vision of a beautiful sunset. It was nice, but I didn't see why God would go out of His way to show this particular picture to me. I asked to see more. Immediately the picture zoomed in and refocused. This time I could see what looked like vast fields of wheat surrounding a great big sun on the horizon that had a blazing cross in the center. The voice of God echoed through the landscape: "The Cross of Christ has become the Throne of Christ Forever!" Next the scene zoomed in again, and as it refocused I could see the throne of Jesus established on the earth shining like the sun. There were millions of people in worship all around it stretching out as far as I could see. As I looked and listened, I began to see that every group of these people was clad in its own unique traditional dress. I heard gorgeous music in a heavenly harmony unprecedented on earth! Every tongue was worshipping in its native language with orchestras playing their own distinctive traditional instruments. I stood in rapture watching and listening to the beautiful panoply of human life and culture arrayed in song with the color of scarves, banners and flags of every description waving in the brilliance. This was a vivid scene straight out of the Bible. This was the great pageant of worship from every nation, tongue and tribe. I saw in that moment that this is the call and destiny of the house of prayer centers in the earth -- to make the name of Jesus known to the ends of the earth; to preserve a remnant in the earth as the reward for His suffering; and to help present the beauty and color of the peoples of the earth as worship to Him and Him alone on that great day.

2011 -- Breakthrough in Prayer

Now two years had passed and I found myself weeping in front of my apartment window again. I was calling out to God with every fiber of my being for the fulfillment of every promise. Far from angry with God, I felt a deep sense of failure in the face of an immense calling and great revelation -- yet with no movement, no victory, and so little success. It was crushing. Even so, God had never been far away. Even in this long season of weeping I felt His presence drawing sharply close. As I wept and prayed on one particular day I began to see each part of God's plan for the house of prayer as He had shown it to me light up, segment by segment, fitted together like a wheel in my mind's eye. I saw His end-time purposes for the House of Prayer stretch out before me like a historical diorama. The whole vision was encircled by the now familiar frame: houses of prayer lit up like points of light around a diagram of the Pacific Rim in sharp relief. Yes, this was the vision that had fuelled my every effort for over ten years now.

As I looked into the vision I mused: This was the dream -- but it wasn't my dream. It was God's dream that He had shared with me, my family and our communities over these years. It filled our minds and hearts. Establishing the Presence of God in the house of prayer had become our one life's work. This was the goal. But it was God's goal -- it never had originated with me. In this moment I didn't know whether to love it or to hate it. Yet, as I looked into the wheel I began to see the face of Jesus illuminated within it. He was wearing His crown. His face was shining, and there was fire in His eyes. I knew this face. This was Jesus ready to come back and take His throne!

I broke down and fell to my knees. Weeping even harder I confessed my deepest heart: my unwavering love for Him. Even if He never did any of it I still and always loved Him. I surrendered everything again in total dependence. Through the tears I declared the truth that I had never done any of it for myself. I had only done everything entirely in obedience to Him. I proclaimed that He was my only purpose -- He was my only goal. Now, my heart exposed, broken and utterly surrendered, I expected that this time my defeat meant that I would be passed over. I expected this glorious purpose to be taken from me and given to someone who would be worthy of its greatness -- someone who would be able to bring the vision to success. I had done all I could.

    Suddenly my being was driven through with a bolt of pure light. My body went rigid on the floor as if a million volts of electricity were flooding through it. From out of the light I saw the wheel diagram, but this time with the House of Prayer at the center. It had spokes radiating out all around it: Education, Training, Outreach, Service, Helping Ministry, The Arts, Hospitality, Business, Economic Development, and more. It was the same vision, but in a new skin with the house of prayer at its heart. God then said,

    "I have called you out of your family, your people, your tribe and your nation. I have called you as part of My plan... like Abraham, like Moses, like Noah. Like Abraham you are called to go out -- following a vision of a City not built by hands. Like Moses you are called to assemble and preserve a people who will be called my own. Like Noah you are called to build a big vision -- something that is a new thing in the earth. You are called to build an end-time ark. You will build it according to My plan as I have given it to you. You will build it as a place of empowerment, protection and provision for my people; and I will preserve a remnant in the earth until my return!"

I have been reluctant to share this experience. For these many years I have not shared what God told me here because I did not want to lift myself up as something special. But it is time to tell it. God has established and re-established this call on my life, and for His purposes. My purpose in relating this is to show the emphatic importance of this, an important piece of God's plan for the end times. I know that I am not the only one with a call like this. There are many emerging with a call to this and other parts of God's end time plan. At this point God finished with a startling commission:

> "Write the plan down on paper. Write it according to the plan that I have given you. Write it down so that it will be made plain to those who read it. Write this plan for the house of prayer centers in the form of a business plan. Build them as centers for community -- including education, outreach, arts, services and businesses -- with the house of prayer at the heart."

I was shocked. I had never written anything like a business plan, and I was certain that I could never do any of the numbers. Frightened at the prospect, I said, "God! You know that I can't write a business plan!" He replied, "I will be with you. I will help you. You will write My plan as a business plan."

With this impossible proclamation settled in heaven and on earth, I did the only thing that I could do. I began to write out the House of Prayer plan, against all earthly possibility, as a business plan. Trying to encapsulate God's vision into the one-page executive summary I wrote a three-page Vision Statement. How can you simplify the purposes of God onto one page? Forging ahead, trying to heed the injunctions of the business plan gurus to keep it short, the thing blossomed into a 60-page document. I was under an open heaven! While I wrote, God talked to me about building it as a hub with all the parts in place. Each hub would be connected to the other hubs, and they will spawn the establishment of other regional and local hubs. He told me that each center would not necessarily look like the others. It had to be built like tinker toy segments, but the whole center in each location would look like the local culture, be built around local strengths, focus on local needs, and carry the DNA of the people and the land. From the foundation it had to be structured to nurture local people leading local teams for local purposes and raising up local leadership to carry out the local vision. God shared so much with me at that time. The plan flowed out in the form of a Development Prospectus complete with vision statement, functional diagram, Business Plan, Financials, Grant Proposals, Development Strategy, Concept Sketches and more.

    Numbers and all, writing the whole plan took me one week. I couldn't believe it! God had to have helped me to write it. It was a miracle. I couldn't believe that I wrote the financials -- and I couldn't believe that they seemed to work! I have never been able to do any level of math, and am thrilled to testify of God's great faithfulness. He miraculously helped me to write a business plan with a full set of financials!

    As soon as the business plan was finished I was incredulous, but also excited. Dionne was exultant of God's great miracle-working power. She intimately knows my utterly lacking math skills! At first I sent it out to a few people who knew something about business. My father told me it was astonishing. A business development consultant I know in Canada said that he went over the numbers and they seemed solid. Our accountant was enthusiastic, and suggested some investors I might send it to.

Then God told me to send it out to everyone I could think of who might like it, who might help spread the word, or invest in it. So I sent it to Christian leaders, missionaries, pastors and anyone who seemed like they might know anything about ministry, business or investment. The feedback was overwhelmingly positive. The general response was that it was a great new idea, and with a little venture capital it seemed as though there might be a chance to see this plan come to reality.

But right then it was 2011 -- smack in the middle of the most severe worldwide economic crash in recent times, one that had started just three years before. Every investor that was suggested to me returned polite rejection letters. Every reply from an investment site online was encouraging but negative. Local business people and investors that I or friends of the plan approached got a clear message: nobody was getting into new projects because of the extreme depths of the economic downturn. It made sense: so many of my friends in the U.S. were suddenly unemployed, and many were losing their homes. So many that we knew, and many more that became common statistics -- people who lost work and couldn't make ends meet anymore; people who were losing their homes and pulling up stakes to try their luck in another place. It seemed too often that it wasn't any better in the new place. But God was taking care of us in Korea, and for some reason was launching a great new concept in business and ministry in the middle of the worst financial crash imaginable.

One day I got an excited email from a friend of ours, Semisi Naqica, in Fiji. We had met Semisi during our time in the War Room in Canada. At that time he was a young missionary on staff at the local YWAM base in West Kelowna. He came to house of prayer sessions every time he could. He was a fierce young Fijian warrior with a great heart for God. He would snatch up a staff in the prayer room and hop forward across the floor with the staff held high like a spear, shouting a high-pitched war cry: "Yi-Yi-Yi-Yi!"! That was Semisi in intercession. He was fiery, whole hearted and utterly lovable. When I shared with him at that time about the house of prayer vision that we carried, he cried out: "I want this for my people! I want this for my land!"

So when I got his email these years later I was thrilled to hear from him. I was even more excited as he told about reading the business plan and he and his wife's amazing heart response. They wrote that they had read the business plan all the way through with tears. They were rejoicing before God that someone was carrying such a vision, and they wanted to bring it to their people. In that email they invited us to come to Fiji. They wanted us to meet pastors and leaders there, they wanted to introduce us to their family and tribe, and they wanted to take us to select places to look at available property. We had our first invitation to establish God's plan!

Chapter 13
God's Glory in the Nations

We were on the flight to Fiji from South Korea. It had been a long flight over oceans of pitch blackness. I had slept a little, but now my legs were cramping and keeping me awake. I didn't want to disturb Dionne sleeping next to me, so I sat and listened to the steady breathing of the blissfully slumbering passengers all around me. I suddenly felt my heart leap -- it was immediately full of song. Wondering, I quietly slid the window shade open and stared out into the darkness with this inexplicable joy flooding my soul. The blackness outside was thick and inky. It was impenetrable – I could see nothing. Then all at once there was a blinding flash of light over a blue and green horizon, and as my eyes adjusted from utter darkness to glorious light, I could see the main island of Fiji below. The chorus that reverberated in my heart was joined by millions of angels that were flying in on channels of this golden light. The scene was brilliant, overwhelming and absolutely gorgeous -- and I suddenly knew two things: Fiji is a portal of heaven for every new day's blessings, and God was soon to bring the people and the land of Fiji into a Golden Jubilee! I knew it with every particle of my body, soul and spirit -- God is going to release the land to the people of the land in Fiji! The angelic traffic came down thick and fast in ordered arrays into the flash of color that is Viti Levu, and out to the rest of the world. My body shivered with the majestic sight which folded into the absolute knowledge that God is going to bless this people: their crops, their land, their new businesses, their children, their families, their culture and their society. God is just waiting for the people to turn to Him, because He can barely hold back the overwhelming blessings that He has prepared for this people and this land! My heart was bursting with the song of the angels, the utter joy of the spectacle and with the glory of God's presence! As we got off the plane I said to Dionne: "Do you feel it?" and then together we cried out, "It's Jubilee"!

We were met at the airport by Semisi and his wife Gela. After a joyful reunion they took us to an apartment in Nadi that they had rented for the four of us during the week of our stay. After settling in, Semisi was fairly bursting with all he had vision for us to do during this trip. "But first," he solemnly intoned, "We have to go meet the Chief!" He explained to us that we would be coming in through the people and in the way of the land. He tried to explain the intricacies of local custom and protocol. It was good enough for me that he understood it and would be leading us through it. This was my first introduction to indigenous protocol and the importance of coming in low and slow… honoring the people of the land as we come. I now insist on coming in anywhere in this way -- through invitation, giving honor and finding the traditional path to come alongside a native people and learn about their ways. Honoring the people of the land in this way is the only way to come in through the spiritual gates established by God in any land on earth. As Jesus said, "…anyone who does not enter the sheep pen by the gate, but climbs in by some other way, is a thief and a robber. The one who enters by the gate is the shepherd of the sheep." John 10:1, 2.

We took a bus from our apartment and walked into a large village full of kids and dogs teaming in clutches down the pathways that led around individual houses and out into a central clearing. Semisi was explaining that this was one of the largest villages in the Nadi area, and we needed to have the blessing of the Chief to come into the land properly. We didn't know just what this meant, but we were up for the adventure. Some of the kids fell in with our small group as we passed. They smiled curiously up at us, a little girl taking Dionne's hand, as if leading us on toward an unknown goal. Semisi stopped at a humble but prominent concrete house among the many wood and bamboo buras (traditional Fijian houses) scattered around. Banana trees clustered around the building and tall palm trees swayed in the late morning sunshine. Semisi called at the door and we were led through the door curtain into a small living room.

    Sitting on plaited mats in the corner of the room was a large Fijian man, smiling as brightly as sunshine. We were introduced and formally gave a gift to the Chief. He quietly asked why we had come. We answered simply that we wanted to bring the house of prayer to Fiji. Abruptly he said, "We don't need explanations; we should just worship the Lord!" A small boy brought a broken guitar held together with duct tape, and the Chief strummed out the most beautiful and resonant chord. They sang in Fijian while the Chief's wife and children gathered into our circle on the grass mats on the floor. The sound filled the house and drew more children from the footpaths outside. Everyone sang in rich harmony. We joined our hearts in worship and sang along with the heavenly sound. We didn't know the tune or the words, but the radiance of worship is the same anywhere you go. You just enter in. We sang and clapped along, laughing and crying in the sheer glory filling the village. The music rose to a heart-rending crescendo, and BOOM! Thunder shook the house as rain poured in sheets outside the open windows. The children shrieked, but the Chief and his wife were laughing. The Chief shouted out over the crashing and clashing of rain and thunder, "What more can I say? The heavens have responded… the earth has responded… God receives our worship and I can only welcome you into the land! We welcome you to Fiji!"

We left the village after tea and crackers at the Chief's house. The downpour had abated. Over the next couple days Semisi took us to meet many pastors and Chiefs in the Nadi area. We travelled around the island, visiting lovely villages, looking at beautiful properties and speaking at a church or two. In Semisi's village of Nadala we had a warm family welcome as we were greeted in a frenzy of flower wreaths and powder thrown on our heads. Evidently, honored guests are powdered as a token of respect. We drove through the waterfall on Mount Tomanivi, we walked through mature jungle to pray over the tribe's ancient sites, we prayed and prophesied over the people and the land. We met with a senator, one of the high Chiefs of Fiji, and shared vision and purpose. This first visit to Fiji was wonderful... and we learned so much.

It was on this first trip that we learned about coming into the people and the land with local protocol, through honor and respect. God reminded me of the times He had told me "Look for the power I have hidden among the least" and "The key to the land is the people of the land." I began to put God's direction together with our new experience, and began to realize the last component of our call. We had always ministered to the least and the disenfranchised; God had always led us to the hurting, the broken and the needy. But now we began to realize that He wanted to plant this revolutionary new plan among the indigenous peoples! He wants to use the power of the least to bring the people and the land together *into their destiny*! God has not forgotten the people of the land: the people who have been downtrodden, beaten, taken advantage of. God has not forgotten the people who have been enslaved by colonial powers, abused and stolen from and then pushed aside, outside of the society of prosperity that has been built on *their stolen inheritance*! God has not forgotten them, and He has a secret plan to make them central to His redemptive end-time plan! This concept of lifting up the people of the land has become central to everything we do.

One week after returning home to Korea from this trip, I got a call from Fiji. The government was impressed with my business plan, and the Prime Minister and his cabinet wanted to meet me. I had to come back to Fiji! Semisi told me that this would also be the perfect time to have an official ceremonial meeting with his brother the Chief of his tribe. I had met with Chiefs already, and I knew I needed to bring a gift!

What do you give to a Chief who has everything? I prayed and researched what to give to a Fijian Chief, but the answers seemed strange. I had a difficult time with it, but over a week I had found it: the perfect whale's tooth! Yes -- the ultimate gift for that certain special Fijian Chief is a whale's tooth. It is the "Tabua", the most coveted of traditional ceremonial gifts.

Once I got back to Fiji we went directly up the mountain to meet the Chief. I was swept up in the traditional "Dua-Dua" ceremony. It is the ceremony of coming into the people and the land. During much oration in their tribal language and crouching on plaited mats, the Tabua was produced. It was held up to the Chief, everyone clapping solemnly three times, with Semisi's mother -- the queen of her people -- beaming beside the Chief. Immediately a "lovo" feast was brought in and served to the whole family, the capstone of the ceremony. I was enchanted, but a little muddled. Something felt different, and I kept asking the family, "What just happened?" Semisi's sister-in-law sat down across from me and said simply,

"You're one of us now!"

After being received by the tribe and granted land to build the house of prayer, Semisi and I travelled down off the mountain to Suva with a retinue of chiefs and pastors to meet with government representatives. I received a warm welcome in meetings among individual cabinet members, with great interest expressed all around. By the end of the day of meetings, the Prime Minister sent his regrets that he had not been able to break away from government business in order to meet with me. He asked if I could stay for another week in hopes that he could find time. I had to send my reply that my flight was due out of Nadi the next day. Even so, it was a fruitful time forging relationships with government officials along with chiefs, pastors and tribal members. Plans were finally being laid for the establishment of the first house of prayer center among tribal people who needed it most!

Myanmar

About the same time I was contacted online by a young man from Burma. The country was still closed at the time, suffering under a horrific absolute communist dictatorship. This young man had found Jesus among the ruins that his nation had become, and was now secretly studying at an underground Bible school in Rangoon. He expressed a fervent heart for his people, a northern hill tribe in the far north of Burma. He emailed or messaged me online almost every evening, asking me the tough questions about life, the Bible, the reality of Jesus, and God's sovereignty in the midst of hardship. I answered as clearly and lovingly as I could, knowing that this young man was living out the answers in ways I couldn't even begin to understand. He had an insatiable hunger for the Truth, and a clear and overwhelming mission: to bring the gospel to his people, the Palaung, an almost totally unreached people group most of whom had never heard the good news of life in Christ. He pleaded with me in his texts and over Skype to come to his land and help him reach out to his people who needed Christ so desperately.

Stephen regularly messaged me for over a year, changing his email address and online identity often in order to avoid the censors in his country and the resulting visit from the national police. But suddenly, in the midst of all this, Burma overthrew the communist dictatorship, changed its name to Myanmar and the capital city became Yangon. I hadn't heard from Stephen for a few months, and was praying for his safety in the midst of the turmoil. Finally he emailed me from Thailand. One of the first changes the new government made was to allow its citizens limited movement outside the country for the first time in decades. Stephen had almost immediately travelled to Chiang Mai and enrolled in a Christian university. He was taking linguistics and forming a team that would translate the Bible into his native Palaung. He quickly invited me to come and meet him in Chiang Mai.

My relationship with Stephen blossomed now that we could spend some time together. From the first he was insistent that I come with him to the Palaung lands and help him preach the gospel to his people. At first, travel into Myanmar was limited to the capital city… the next year most of the main cities were open, as long as visitors were travelling with an official tour group. Stephen and I kept meeting and praying together, laying plans for our trip into Palaung territory as soon as it was possible. Presently I was reading blog accounts of individual travellers who were ignoring the travel restrictions and trekking into the back country in Myanmar. I wasn't sure I was up for it, but Stephen assured me that it would be safe. Now the major towns were open all over the country, and many backpackers were hiking into the mountains.

So we set a date and I met Stephen in Lashio. Lashio is a frontier town in the far North of Shan State. It is surrounded by hill tribe areas all around, and is the last town North before the Chinese border. Lashio is very rustic, to say the least, but it is the regional center because it is a market town where many hill tribe people and Chinese businessmen come to trade and sell their wares. It is a small town lacking in some services and many of the conveniences of modern life, but that is part of its beautiful, unique, rural charm!

While the plane was flying into Lashio, God told me to go to Deuteronomy 32. I immediately began to pray this portion, and in that moment God opened my mind to a completely new understanding. On that small propeller plane with tribal people dressed in their traditional costumes belted in around me -- God gave me the message of the Destiny of Nations. The next day I proclaimed this word over the people and the land at a Baptist church service, "Let this teaching fall like rain, and my words descend like dew, like showers on new grass, like abundant rain on tender plants" (vs. 2). As I proclaimed these words thunder rolled and heavy rain began to fall. They told me later that this rainfall had broken a three year drought in the area.

I went on to preach that God has "...given the nations their inheritance..." (vs. 8) and as part of that inheritance He has given each nation a unique destiny. To grasp that destiny God's instructions are to: "Remember the days of old; consider the generations long past. Ask your father and he will tell you, ask your elders, and they will explain to you" (vs. 7). By looking into the history, the land, the culture and the ancient stories we will be able to see and understand the unique character of a people and begin to grasp their end-time destiny. Part of the work of the house of prayer is to grab hold of the destiny of the people and to lift up the people of the land so that the people and the land can step into this destiny. I preached this message first in Lashio, but it has become central to the message God has me bring whenever I am invited into a new land, among a new people.

The next day Stephen and I met early in order to travel into Palaung territory. Our destination was six hours away, through the jungle and up a mountain. Stephen showed up on his small motorbike in front of my guesthouse in Lashio. I asked him if I needed to rent a car or truck for the trip. He replied that there was no car or truck we could rent in Lashio. I asked him if I needed to rent a motorbike like his to get us on our way. He replied that there was no motorbike for us to rent in Lashio. Astonished, I asked him what we would do? He smiled and gently patted the back end of the motorbike's seat.

    After situating my overnight bag between Stephen's legs, I jumped on to the back of his small motorbike. The "motorbike", as they call them all over Asia, is not a motorcycle as people in Western countries know them. It is something more akin to a small dirt bike, somewhat larger than a scooter. It has a small frame with a small, extremely fuel efficient engine. This engine must not have been much bigger than 100 ccs. So, two large men rode away on a small motorbike, with me hanging on dearly to the bar on the back. We sped out of Lashio and onto a local road crowded over on both sides with dense jungle.

    We sped through jungle that stood in water as though it were a vast overgrown lake. We sped through small villages which opened onto rice fields. We sped for hours on a lonely road heading toward the tall mountains. Always toward the tall peaks in the distance. We stopped once at a tea house, and then on the road again. At great length we reached a wide river which marked the boundary into Palaung territory. The road on the far side of the river went straight up the side of the mountain! Only -- there was no road. Once we crossed the bridge to the other side of the river we found a "road" made up of gravel and rock interspersed with large chunks of broken concrete. Stephen expertly threaded his way between the biggest rocks and chunks, but the back of the motorbike was tossing me up and down severely. I quickly learned to ride the back of that bike like a horseman at full gallop. The motorbike climbed in fits and starts straight up the track, climbing up and still upward around forested bends and across small waterfalls that flowed over the rocky path. We travelled up and up, past young men with hollow stares clutching machine guns in their hands; past a small army troop, past roaring cries in the jungle, past tea plantations high on cloud shredding peaks.

We were simply told to leave when we got there. Apparently the war was raging and it wasn't safe for a foreigner to be up in the mountains. So we prayed over the land, proclaimed the Name of YHWH over the people and the land, and established a spiritual foothold over more than 2 million people who have yet to hear the name of Jesus. Since then we have been up into the mountains of the Palaung territory a handful of times, have rented a traditional shop as a refugee center and have been given a piece of land to build a permanent outreach center among this lost and war-torn people.

Chapter 14
The Glory Continues

On our trips to Lashio I met Pastor Kyaw Kyaw, the Director of Shan Regional Evangelical Bible Institute, SREBI. In fact, he translated the message for me the day I arrived and first preached *The Destiny of Nations*. He told me afterward that translation that day was extremely difficult: he didn't know whether I was proclaiming the word, preaching the word or prophesying the word. It was all three. He has become a valued friend and partner, and I have been back to teach at SREBI. This Bible school is unique because it is founded in Lashio, a regional hub for scores of hill tribe peoples. Ministering in Lashio is strategic to ministering into these groups. Part of the main purpose at SREBI is to minister into the remote tribal villages and bring back a few who feel called to study the Bible at SREBI. Then SREBI helps them get back into their villages to set up churches and outreach ministries.

The students at SREBI are so precious. Young people called by the Lord, with a fire to bring the gospel back to their own people. It's not an easy road. Life in the villages is very basic. These young pastors return to minister precisely to the people who cannot afford to pay them. The villagers build a small house and church out of bamboo and mud, give tithes and offerings in chickens and local produce, and the young ministers pray to survive; and to make a difference among their people with the hope of the Gospel.

On a recent visit to SREBI I was honored to teach in their new facilities. Built by hand with concrete block, metal roofing and lumber logged from the property, it has been a labor of love by Pastor Kyaw Kyaw and a small team of local builders. SREBI has set aside a portion of land to build a house of prayer in conjunction with the school in partnership with us. They have a vision to establish tribal house of prayer outreach centers that will work to lift up the people of the land. SREBI is building, teaching and ministering by faith, so that the local hill-tribe people of far Northern Shan State can hear the Truth, believe and build a new life in Christ. Slowly their ministry is lifting up the people.

South India

A number of years ago we met a pastor from Coimbatore, South India. Pastor Raj came to Korea to attend a conference on missions in South and Central Asia. When we met him he was finished with the conference but reluctant to return home. He felt that God had something more for him while he was here in Korea. When we met, the topic of the house of prayer seemed to come up immediately. He was looking for more of what God wanted to do for his region. We took him to a corner coffee shop and told him about the house of prayer -- its purpose, practice and calling. He was fascinated, and it just so happened that we were on our way to help lead a house of prayer session at a local church. We asked him along.

That night was especially powerful as God prophetically led us to open up the session and have people bring their hurts, fears, sins and disappointments to the altar. We turned a large cymbal over as a receptacle and encouraged any who would come, to write down what they needed to bring and let go of on the altar of God's redemptive fire. The prophetic act left Pastor Raj speechless after the session.

Through tears he asked for our information so that we could stay in touch.

Pastor Raj reports that after he got home he excitedly told his church about the concept of the house of prayer. He immediately established a house of prayer session on Thursdays. The first session they had no worship leader, so they simply sang and prayed for their church and their neighborhood. As they prayed a woman cried out with a burden for her son -- a young man who had been saved in childhood, but was now living a fast and loose lifestyle on the wild streets of India. As the group joined in and began to pray for this woman's son, the young man came storming into the church. He stomped up the aisle telling everyone that God would not let him alone; He had compelled him to come to the church. The group knew this was a miracle, and lovingly gathered around the boy. They prayed for him and he was delivered of alcohol and set free from drugs that night. Joyfully, he picked up a guitar and led worship for the group through the night.

From then on the young man was the worship leader for the Thursday night meeting. As weeks went by the worship became more and more free. Prophecy began to come forth over the people from among the ranks of the regular attendees, and soon healings started to manifest. It did not take long until worship, intercession and revelation was met with salvation, deliverance, healing and new lives for many. As Pastor Raj tells it, soon some of these people's Hindu friends started hearing about what was happening. They asked, "You just sing songs and people are healed, delivered and set free?" The Christians told their friends,

"Yes! Why don't you join us?" But the Hindus said that they couldn't attend a Christian church in the Christian neighborhood. It wouldn't look right to their Hindu friends. But they came up with an idea:

"Come, bring your singing to our house in the Hindu neighborhood once a month, and we can have this too!"

So, the Christians started to bring the house of prayer sessions to the Hindu neighborhood. Now many Hindus were getting saved, delivered and healed. But soon some of the people's Muslim friends started hearing about what was happening. They asked, "You just sing songs and people are healed, delivered and set free?" The Christians told their friends,

"Yes! Why don't you join us?" But the Muslims said that they couldn't attend a Christian church in the Christian neighborhood. It wouldn't look right to their Muslim friends. But the Muslims asked:

"Don't you come to sing in the Hindu neighborhood? Come, bring your singing to one of our houses in the Muslim neighborhood once a month, and we can have this too!"

So, the Christians and the new Hindu converts started to bring the house of prayer sessions to the Muslim neighborhood. Soon many Muslims were getting saved, delivered and healed. Now Pastor Raj reports that they have a mobile house of prayer that moves every week from the Christian neighborhood to the Hindu neighborhood and then to the Muslim neighborhood. Most recently they have pooled their resources and bought a parcel of land that stands sandwiched in between all three neighborhoods on the edge of town. It was chosen as being suitable for any of the local residents to visit. They have asked us to help them establish a house of prayer there, on that land. They have called it City of God House of Prayer Coimbatore.

Thailand

In Thailand we met an unbridled group of intense worshippers who practice the presence of God in absolute surrender to the Holy Spirit. This isn't strange to me, but to find it among a raw group of relatively new believers ministering in impoverished circumstances among the very least, in a country filled with the least, was shockingly and breathtakingly beautiful. These weren't people experimenting with going after God from the comfort of their beautiful facilities and luxurious homes, these were people running after His presence because it was all they valued. They pursue the One Thing and experience His power in the midst of their absolute need, in the midst of the dirt -- slain in the Spirit in a small storefront church and communal home, or under metal sheeting in the middle of a pasture. They eat when God provides. Otherwise they fast and pray. They don't own homes, but are now living in tents and building a new church with their hands. Pastors Yadah and Wadee have given over their lives to God 100%, bringing to Thai people the power of God to come out of alcoholism, abusive families, massage parlors and worse. They are full of the joy and power of the Holy Spirit, and the whole community immediately responded to the word we brought.

Since we met these wild and amazing, abandoned worshippers they have followed hard after the concept of the house of prayer, establishing several house of prayer sessions a week in their church. When we met them they had formed a small church in Bo Win, an area outside Pattaya. Soon after, they were planting seven churches in remote areas and networking with even more. Now they have built a network of over 30 churches that they have planted or are partnered with, and all of them are crying out to establish houses of prayer. Partnered with these beautiful hearts, we have the opportunity to plant houses of prayer all over Thailand. They can't pay anything to help us come to them, but we still go none-the-less.

Cambodia

A diminutive powerhouse of a pastor contacted me online from Cambodia. Soly Yun eagerly expressed his heart to establish the house of prayer in his rural area in Cambodia. When I went to see him I was not ready for what I would find. He pastors a small church which he built by hand from concrete blocks, and cares for almost thirty orphans. Up to this point they all lived in the church building and in a small house built alongside. They bathe and eat outside along with geese, ducks and chickens. They eat the local produce along with what they can raise.

Besides pastoring a church and raising a troop of orphans, Soly treks out into even more remote areas to reach out to local villages. He showed me water wells he had dug and introduced me to the new believers. I taught a simple lesson in small English classes Soly has organized for the village children, but the whole village stands alongside mouthing the words and trying out the exercises.

Soly and the orphans have now moved into a new facility, thanks to partial government funding and the love of Christians around the world. They still have pressing ongoing needs -- and God faithfully provides – but there is so much more that Soly wants to accomplish for the many more orphans in need of a home. They also have set aside a plot of land to build a house of prayer. But the most pressing need in their rural location is education. There is virtually no source of quality education in Soly's area, and there are no Christian schools. Soly dreams of building a Christian school that will impact his whole region for Christ. He has asked for our help, and we have the knowledge and expertise, but Soly needs investment for his school. Is there anyone who would want to impact virtually a whole province in Cambodia with the Gospel?

Ministering Among the "Least of These"

An important point of all these stories is that God has spoken to us about reaching out to the very least in the earth with the power of worship, intercession and revelation. He has called us to lift up the people of the land with the power of His Presence -- this often means that we are called to minister to the poorest, the neediest, and the most vulnerable. Orphans in Cambodia, war refugees in Palaung territory, tribal villagers and ex-trafficked people in Thailand desperately need the comfort of the Holy Spirit and the Presence of God established in their neighborhoods in the house of prayer. Yet for virtually all of the people that we work with, they cannot afford to pay for us to come and minister to them. For us there are no flight vouchers, no big honorariums and no hotels with banquet facilities. The people to whom we minister give what they can, and share everything they have.

On ministry trips I have been provided lodging in Korean sex motels, on a woven mat in a Fijian Bura, in a Thai brothel, in bamboo huts in countless villages, under a Burmese industrial turbine to try to foil the sweltering heat, in the Chief's mother's bed (she was the only one who had an actual bed), and yes, also occasionally in hotel rooms. I have eaten everything including Korean silkworm larvae, live ocean worms, Burmese pig's feet, tea plucked fresh from the bushes, sashimi filleted right off the living, gaping fish, Chinese chicken feet, pickled centipedes... and much more. I contracted typhoid twice and almost died in a Korean hospital. These stories are not intended as boasting or for shock value. They are briefly related here to highlight the fact that we have had to take the initiative ourselves to follow God's guidance and go; to use whatever income we could in order to minister into many countries on a small personal budget. Yet I wouldn't trade any of it for the world -- God continues to provide. In Fiji, among the Palaung, in Lashio, in Thailand, in Cambodia and so many places we work we have land already given for the purpose of building house of prayer centers among the people and in the land. But in many of these areas the government won't make land use approvals, even in extremely rural areas, without an initial investment.

Our Call: The Purpose, Vision and Mission

In the bigger picture, these centers will be planted in order that God's end-time plan will be established and facilitated among the peoples who would most benefit. Right now, these centers must be planted to reach unreached peoples, to call Christians up worldwide and teach that there is a deeper purpose to which God is calling us. They need to be planted to equip groups of believers to go to the profound power of the One Thing: the relationship that God is seeking with us, so that we can be radically changed and empowered to do the things Jesus said that we will do -- in every corner of the globe. These centers need to be planted so that men and women will come to learn to effect change in heavenly places, and go from these centers empowered to effect that change in their world. These centers will be established as outposts of Heaven's Kingdom on Earth, and God wants to do it among the tribal peoples.

But, further, these centers must be established in key sites around the world because God has promised a massive global revival and harvest in Habakkuk 2:14, Isaiah 60:1-5, Acts 2:17, and many other passages throughout the Bible. This outpouring will reach every nation, tongue and tribe. These centers will be necessary to this end-time move of God as staging areas for the prophesied outpouring, as mobilization centers from which the massive work is to move out, and as supply centers for ongoing activation and provisioning. This outpouring will be birthed in individual hearts as we receive a revelation of God's radical love and absolute power, and then move throughout the world as we apprehend this love and power and respond in extravagant worship, passion and acts of service poured out before His throne and into the streets.

These centers must be established because they will be cities of refuge for Christians and for a wounded and broken world. We need these centers established in order to reach out to the homeless, the hungry, and the enslaved – spiritually and physically. These centers will be places of shelter, of provision and of opportunity for many who need them – jobs for people coming out of poverty or the sex trade -- with small enterprise opportunities supported by, and in turn supporting the central purposes of worship, intercession and revelation, and the complimentary functions of teaching, training, evangelism and support ministries. These centers will be lands of Goshen for God's people -- they will be places of light in the darkness; blessing in the midst of chaos; provision in the middle of great need.

The vision is to build communities of prayer housed in high-quality multi-function centers that will be equipped to teach, train and mentor worshippers, intercessors, prophets and teachers into local areas; to release worship, intercession and revelation in every expression – especially in the area of the arts; to mobilize 5-fold teams who will travel out to help build vision and practical ability in local groups; to help local groups establish affiliated centers; to create and distribute resource materials.

The mission is to build a network of flagship centers among indigenous people groups which will develop regional networks throughout their parts of the world; to see equipping centers with houses of prayer at their core established in strategic locations around the world in order to equip the body of Christ, help set the stage for the end-time outpouring, and be built up as cities of refuge. It is not incidental to God's plan that they be made comfortable and beautiful.

There is a paramount urgency to begin this work: God has shown us that this establishment must be in place, in order to fulfill much of the prophecy concerning Christ's second coming: "I will establish Zion" (Psalm 87), "that all the gentiles may come and seek the Lord" (Micah 4). The establishment of worldwide education, service and economic centers with houses of prayer at their core is key to facilitating the preparation of the body of Christ, serving God's end-time outpouring, and setting the stage for Christ's ultimate return to establish His Kingdom on earth.

The End?

So now the book has an ending. Sort of. It is an ending that is still in progress. The story is still unfolding in eight nations now, with more invitations almost every day. We speak where we are invited. We travel where the door opens. We minister among people who feel their need for God quite tangibly. They are some of the hungriest people in the world -- they just want God! The work is blessed, and God is extremely satisfying in the midst of it. So it is exciting to let you know that you too can be a part of this amazing end time work among the very least in the earth!

We offer an invitation: Come along on the adventure! There are many ways you can become a part. You could sign up for our prayer bulletins. You might make a donation. You could become an active fundraiser among your own communities in your area. You can tell about the work we are doing to your friends, to potential investors, to funding agencies. You could tell pastors in your local area about us and arrange invitations for us to come speak at churches. You might partner with us and join our internship program in Korea, Cambodia or Myanmar. You could make an investment in one of our projects. But most of all, you can commit to pray for us and our work. The message here came to us in prayer. This growing international network was birthed in prayer, and has only moved forward by being bathed in years of constant tears, intercession and crying out to God. We so appreciate all of those who have joined hearts and hands with us to push forward in prayer. In any way you may be able, we extend the invitation: *Come along on the adventure!*

Ch 15 The Call to The House of Prayer

God has told us throughout His word that He would do a major work in the earth in these last days. In Acts 15, James quotes the prophet Amos, *" 'After these things I will return, and I will rebuild the tabernacle of David which has fallen, and I will rebuild its ruins, and I will restore it, so that the rest of mankind may seek the LORD, and all the Gentiles who are called by my Name,' says the LORD who makes these things known from long ago" Acts 15:16, 17 & 18*. The establishment of Houses of Prayer, springing up today all over the world, is a direct fulfillment of this promise God made long ago.

A Word of Warning

At this point my heart is moved to offer a gentle word of warning. Do not pray and intercede that the darkness be turned back on your main streets unless you intend to set up the light once the darkness is rolled away. Many earnest hearts network to pray earnestly against a New Age bookstore, or a dubious business or some such thing in their town, when no one intends to raise up any establishment of light and truth in its place. Don't we know that faith without works is dead[1]? We can pray and take dominion over darkness, but if that dominion is not for the purpose of establishing the light in the earth, God's Kingdom establishment, then our dominion is of no use, and without fruit.

Jesus himself tells us that if one evil spirit is driven out, that one and seven more will come back and take up residence if the land is left unoccupied: *if an establishment of the Spirit of God is not erected in its place*[2]! Our cities reflect this. Many have spent much time and

---

[1] James 2:17.
[2] Matt. 12:43-45.

effort praying, writing letters, circulating prayer requests and petitions, organizing prayer meetings and initiatives "weeding" their communities of darkness, but if we do not then plant an establishment of the light of the Kingdom in the place of the establishment of darkness, we are only wearying ourselves, wasting our time and efforts, and preparing the ground for an ever greater harvest of spiritual darkness.

In this way traditional religion has acted like the kings of old who established the works of God but did not pull down the high places of idolatry. They had a little blessing, but without power. These kings were overcome.

On the other hand, the results of zeal and intercession alone have been like the kings who pulled down the high places but did not establish the works of God in their place. These kings reaped some benefits but could not grasp a lasting peace. These kings were also overcome.

We must be like the very few of the ancient Hebrew kings who actively pulled down the high places of darkness and also intentionally established the word of the Lord, the House of Prayer, and other Kingdom establishments in their societies. Only then will we, like King David and a very few others open the power of the blessings of God with a lasting peace.

The world is only planting houses of New Age spiritism on Main Street because their hearts hunger and thirst for Spirit and Truth to be founded there. We must have the courage to establish Houses of Prayer dedicated to worship, intercession and revelation right in the midst of our cities where the seeker, the lost and the hurting can find them.

Certainly we must pray! Of course we must take dominion. But then we must use that dominion to establish the light. Replace New Age bookstores, houses of fortune tellers and nightclubs on Main Street with the House of Prayer partnered with Kingdom bookstores, healing rooms, coffee houses, multi-media worship celebrations, worship art galleries, and more in their place.

In this way the words of Proverbs 2:21, 22 will come to pass, when "...the upright do inhabit the earth, and the perfect are left in it, and the wicked from the earth are cut off, and treacherous dealers plucked out of it!" (Young's Literal Translation).

Oh God, make Your body salt and light. Call her, call her to be salty. Call her to establish the light in Houses of Prayer that You desire and that the world cries out for.

Conclusions

God is in the process of fulfilling His promise of restoring the Tabernacle of David in the earth in order to accomplish His end-time purposes. This is the House of Prayer movement, which is quietly sweeping communities all over the world. The power of this move of God is in the establishment of the pattern of heaven in the earth, which has always been His strategy from before time, and throughout history.

The foundational structure that the LORD has revealed for the establishment of the House of Prayer is the structure of the Three-Strand Cord: Worship, Intercession, and Revelation. These functions are the work of heaven in the earth: the work of the priesthood. This structure is the veritable DNA at the core of everything that is part of the House of Prayer.

The pattern for the government and operation of the Kingdom that God has desired for His people throughout the ages is a pattern of priestly functions: a kingdom of priests, each operating in his own area of gifting, in relationship to the rest of the body, with God Himself as the head. The varied functions of the House of Prayer, however distinct, must operate together as a whole, as a team of teams. This cannot be accomplished by the plan or purpose of any person; it must be by the orchestration of the Spirit of God.

The priestly pattern of the function of the House of Prayer further reinforces the foundational necessity of vertical and horizontal relationship as the basis for the structure and function of the House of Prayer. This is the pattern of the cross: laying everything of ourselves down to make intimate, personal relationship with Christ the absolute first necessity in our lives, and relationship with each other in a team structure the second. This relational pattern, this pattern of heaven, this pattern of the cross, is the only plan that can contain the power to effect God's end-time plan for the redemption of His people and the earth.

We are in the time of the restoration of all things. God is restoring this fallen tent of David in the earth. In that, God is calling His people to the faith and practice that He has intended from the foundation of the world. God is showing us a glimmer of an approach to life and ministry where we come together to celebrate the story of God's Love in and through each of us, in His way, on His calendar, based on a pattern of the Tree of Life deeply rooted in the power of His presence. He is calling us, in the establishment of the House of Prayer, to institute a whole and connected approach, an invitation to everyone who wants to join as participants, where we celebrate the story of God's extravagant love for us shown in what He has done, is doing, and will do to redeem us and set us free in the establishment of the Kingdom of God in the earth, operating in the same way that it does in heaven.

God intends to build communities of His people in the earth that will be radical in their commitment to Him, and to each other. This kind of unity will make the Body of Christ into a beacon in the gathering darkness of the kingdoms of this world, like never before seen in the earth. It is volcanic chains of Houses of Prayer throughout regions all over the earth that will usher in this kind of passionate experience of intimacy and unity with the heart of God, and with one another.

The House of Prayer has many faces: bridal chamber, strategy room, community resource center, creative community, and many more. The House of Prayer in a community will take on the unique flavor of the community it is planted in, and at the same time maintain a commitment to the global call of the House of Prayer as a whole.

Implications

This work is about the team. It will only be accomplished through a new revelation to the Body of the importance of working in teams. The work of the priesthood is the work of teams. We must have every function of the priesthood working together. This work must also be relational. We must cultivate a new heart of living in the secret place in the most intimate relationship with Christ, and working that out in relational connection with one another. Community, in fact, is mission-critical to establishing this work. Our notion of community must grow past a notion of casual fellowship, or even of small-group connectedness. Genuine community is most clearly reflected in Jesus' High Priestly prayer in John 17.

The House of Prayer is a work of joining the whole Body in worship, prayer and revelation; it is a work of the joining of streams. It will entail the joining and honoring of all generations, races and nationalities. It will necessitate the gifts and the fruit of the Spirit operating together. We will need all of the various parts of the Body to come together, all of the talents and giftings and emphases, to work together and begin showing forth His image with more completeness.

The House of Prayer is about the merging of worship, prophetic and intercessory strands. It is about celebrating God's presence and moving in the three strands through lavish creative expression. It is about the cultivation of a heart for our brother Israel and the Hebrew roots of our faith. This work is about cultivating a heart for the streets, both in the marketplace and those disenfranchised from the mainstream. It is about a heart for our cities, and standing up for them in the truth. It is about cultivating a heart for God's Justice and Mercy poured out to the weak and the dying in the world.

The House of Prayer and God's End-Time Plan

The greatest reason for the establishment of the House of Prayer is that God is worthy. He is worthy of our worship, our prayers, our time and attention. He is worthy of our hearts' response to His love for us seven days a week, twenty-four hours a day. But God has His own reasons for breathing this vision into so many hearts in cities all over the globe today. The House of Prayer is vital to God's end-time plan for the earth.

Right now darkness is falling like a curtain all over the earth. Western culture is reaching depths of excess, depravity and despair only hinted at throughout history. The darkness of anti-Semitism and anti-Christ is rising on every continent, especially across central Europe. A huge resurgence of Wiccan-styled paganism is flooding countries all over the world, sparked and nurtured by the media in movies, books, popular magazines and many publications for children. Ancient idol worship is on the rise masked as a return to "traditional" culture all over Asia and Africa, but it is also springing up throughout the western world[1].

How can we face an onslaught of darkness as large and pervasive as this? We have not been equipped to face it in our Sunday morning meetings, as wonderful and powerful as many often are. God's plan for battle is the same as it always has been: establish the power and presence of heaven on earth in the midst of the darkness and chaos. This was His plan in the establishment of the Garden of Eden, with His people given rulership over it. This was His plan as He sent Abraham in search of a city not made by hands. This was His plan as He gave the plan of heaven to Moses in the picture of the Tabernacle where His presence would dwell amongst His people. His plan, moreover, is the only plan that will be effective in this darkening hour.

The citadels of the power and presence of heaven that God is calling us to establish in the earth today are Houses of Prayer planted in strategic cities all over the world. It is time for the people of God to arise and shine[2], even as great darkness is falling over the people of the earth. The establishment of the House of Prayer is absolutely vital to God's end-time plan to bring His body together, make ready His Bride, show His Glory through her, and ultimately usher in the return of Christ.

The last prayer of Jesus will be answered through the coming together of churches in the House of Prayer. As churches in an area gain a vision for establishing a House of Prayer in their area, they will be faced with the joy and challenge of pulling together in order to make it happen. As the body of Christ comes together to build this foundation of pure worship, intercession and revelation before the throne of God, they will begin, by necessity and by grace, to come into the unity that has always been in the heart of Christ for the church[3].

---

[1] Isaiah 60:2 is quickly coming to pass!
[2] The necessity for us to respond to Is. 60:1 is growing ever more urgent in direct proportion to the manifestation of the great darkness of Is. 60:2 in the world. The House of Prayer is key to that "arising and shining".

How can we maintain our small differences when we are coming together to worship Him? Through the House of Prayer the door will be opened to a new unity in the body of Christ.

Further, the Bride will be prepared in the flame of the secret place that is at the heart of the House of Prayer. Through the establishment of the House of Prayer the necessary experience of deep intimacy with Christ will be spread throughout the church. Through this fire of intimacy the Bride will step into purity. This heart change within the church will establish love as the foundation within the body of Christ. As a result of this heart change the Bride will receive God's heart for the lost[1]. When she is filled with His intimate presence she will love what He loves and hate what He hates[2]. The Bride of Christ will then be empowered with the power of love and purity to reach out into the world as a city on a hill[3].

As the House of Prayer is established and filled with a renewed and empowered Bride, this city set on a hill will emerge as the prophesied Mount of The LORD[4], shining out into the darkness that the nations may seek Him. As the House of Prayer is established in cities, strongholds of darkness will be broken and cast down. These cities will become citadels of the Kingdom of God, established with the power of the House of Prayer at their core. These Kingdom citadels will operate as cities of refuge, cities of Kingdom authority, and centers for apostolic resource. These apostolic centers will be safe home bases for the Bride throughout the earth, and centers where worship, evangelism, the arts, teaching, and resource will flow out. The establishment of these Kingdom Citadels will be key to a prepared Bride working in the midst of the harvest of souls prophesied at the end of the age[5].

As the heart of the Church is prepared in love and purity within

---

[3] According to John 17 and Eph. 4:13.
[1] I Tim. 2:1-4.
[2] Ps. 97:10; Prov. 8:13.
[3] According to Matt. 5:14.
[4] One instance of this thread of prophecy is found in Zech. 8:20-22, but there are many similar passages too numerous to reference.
[5] Rev. 14:14-16.

the House of Prayer, our hearts will begin to be tuned to the heart of God, turned toward the lost, and toward our brother Israel. Through the establishment of the House of God in the earth giving place for this work of love in the heart of the Church, we will step toward our brother Israel. Israel's heart will be turned in jealousy at that time[1] and God will reveal Messiah Jeshuah to them[2]; restoring the two houses to one another, and making them one staff in His hand.

Finally, this establishment of worship, intercession and revelation, this maturing of the Bride, this outpouring of love within the church, this sovereign work of restoration between the houses of the church and Israel, all will set the stage for God's massive outpouring of His Spirit upon all flesh[3]. At this time the established Houses of Prayer will act as equipping and staging platforms for the wholesale outpouring of God's Spirit on all people throughout the world. The establishment of the House of Prayer throughout the earth in this day is absolutely essential to God's end-time plan as it unfolds for the church, His people Israel, and the nations of the world. The establishment of the House of Prayer, quite possibly in your hometown, is ordained of God as absolutely key to God's end-time purposes throughout the world. We are in a time when God is challenging many of us who have ears to hear to put our hands, hearts and resources to work to see the House of Prayer established in our communities. The House of Prayer is a physical establishment of the work of heaven in the earth. As such it is the seed of heaven planted among us. As long as we will not plant the seed, we will not see the fruit[4]. We all long for God's kingdom to come among us in power[5]. We sing and pray for revival to come, but God is revealing to us an important part of His strategy, foretold throughout the scriptures, for establishing His move in the earth: the restoration of David's tabernacle! The House of Prayer is the seed, the kernel of heaven

---

[1] Rom. 10:19 quotes Moses' words in Deut. 32:21.
[2] Rom. 11:26.
[3] According to Joel 2:28-30.
[4] Mark 4:26-29, I Cor. 3:6 – as Paul first "planted", Apollos "watered", and God gave the increase of fruit.
[5] I Cor. 4:20.

planted in the earth to help prepare His bride, to help equip the body, to contain the power of heaven so that it may begin to flow forth into the world.

Christ could have done it all. Yet He wanted us, the people whom the Spirit of God will prepare in the last days of the world to establish a house in the earth whose purpose is to worship and lift up His name, His kingdom, as it is in heaven. This is the work that will hallow the Name of YHWH in the earth and establish the kingdom of heaven here among us! This Kingdom established among us is the House of Prayer and Worship that the Spirit and our hearts long to establish right now. This is the work that He is establishing among us so that we can begin to make the kingdoms of this world into the kingdoms of Our LORD, and of His Christ, and from this house He will progressively reign, until He reigns all forever and ever!

Jesus could have done it all himself, but he wanted us! He wanted to establish us in the earth, so that He could establish this house in us, so that He could establish His glory in this house, so that He could have us as His glorious Bride participating in His rulership from here into eternity. God the Father is commissioning us, charging us to build this house in this day, so that His glorious Name can be established[1] in a powerful way throughout the earth. We are called to a privilege and a high calling, unprecedented in scope, scale and sheer glory: we are called to the establishment of heaven in the earth, the establishment of the House of Prayer[2]!

This book is the first book in a series on the establishment of the house of prayer. It outlines the foundations for values and beginning structures. The second book, *The Seven Spirits of God* goes further into depth on structures, and sketches out basic practices founded on these foundational values and structures. *The Destiny of*

---

[1] Hab. 2:14.
[2] Tom's End Note: I like what Isaiah says in Chapter 64, vs. 4. Paul makes reference to this portion in I Cor. 2:9 – but doesn't stop there. He continues on in verse 10, " But God has revealed them to us by His Spirit. For the Spirit searches *all things,* yes, the *deep things of God.*" I Cor. 2:10 (Emphasis mine). The restoration of the Tabernacle of David in the House of Prayer in these days is one of those deep things of God. See also Acts 3:20 & 21.

Nations is the name of the third book in the series, fleshing out the call of God on people groups and nations through the end times and the vital role the house of prayer has to play in this, a key part of His end time plan. These three books were originally intended to work together as guides for values, structures and practice in establishing the house of prayer. During the years of writing, however, God has made clear that they apply to all Kingdom structures through the times we are now entering. I am humbled, but also compelled to assert that the truths in these three books apply equally to churches, ministries, businesses, especially to Kingdom structures on the seven mountains of society, communities and families, as well as the house of prayer.

These three books are prophetic sketches of an apostolic structure that God has given to help us live and flourish through the end times and into the establishment of His ultimate rule and reign in the earth. I hear the Spirit of God crying out: "Who will Love?... Who will love God First in everything, and love his neighbor enough to reach out and make this establishment? Who will love... Who will love enough to lay down everything and give all to the establishment of the Kingdom of God in the earth? Who will love... Who will see the ultimate value in this establishment that God is building in the earth – the value to the heart of God, the value to our fellow men and women, the value to regions and nations of the world – the ultimate value in making disciples of all nations and laying at Jesus' feet the reward of His suffering? Who will Love?...

Come Along on the Adventure!

Everything that you find here, and more, is available for teaching, training and equipping. Our team is available to travel and share the vision with any group that is interested. The Development prospectus for the centers is available to anyone who might like to partner with us. Please stand with us by joining the network, investing in any of our center opportunities, praying or donating.

More information is available at: *www.throughtheveil.net*.

For more about the house of prayer: *www.ringoffirehop.org*

For our missions and outreach: *www.pacifichope.org*

For education: *www.pacificgates.org*

For our ongoing work in business development: *www.ringoffireeconomicdevelopment.org*

You can also email us with specific questions or expressions of interest at: *admin@throughtheveil.net*

Come Along on the Adventure!

178

Appendix I
A Final Word

The following was prayed and spoken over me in the War Room on April 8, 2004. It was given in one of the regular War Room prayer sessions by Lisa Hernandez, a missionary to Mexico on sabbatical at the time.

"This is a strategic step, an important step, that the Bride of Christ accepts God's invitation as He is wooing us into His House. Lord, I thank You for what You're doing in the Earth. I thank You for the Age that You have called us to be in, this time, the End of the Age. We just thank You for the beginning of the revelation that You are giving to us: that You are drawing us in, You're drawing us into Your House, You're drawing us in gently by Your Spirit, inviting us to come into Your House. You want us to come in near to You right now.

It's a calling in, a calling in, and I know You are doing it in all the Earth. A calling in of Your Bride, and Your Bride is also calling, saying come in, come into the Temple, come into My House. This is a very, very important time for the Bride of Christ to respond, to respond to the Lord. Now, this is a NOW word to respond to the Lord to come in, to come in and be with the Father; to get His heart, to hear His heart and to be baptized, to be soaked in the Spirit of God. Because when You want to send us out it's not by might or by power but by Your Spirit, and we need to come into that, we need to come into that.

This is such a strategic time for the Bride of Christ to come in. And I just call out to Her to come in, to come into the House. Come into the House of the Father. Respond to the Holy Spirit, He's wooing you Bride of Christ. Come in, come in, come in. Respond *instantly:*

Come! Nothing is more important at this time.

And I ask that You, Jesus, would drop the revelation, drop the revelation on Her, drop the Spirit of Revelation on us the Bride of Christ, to understand that You are calling us in, and that this is a strategic part of the End Time Movement that You are working: that You want to anoint Your Bride. You want to anoint Your Bride and You want to launch Her out. You want to launch Her out into the End Time Harvest. But we don't want to be sent out prematurely without the anointing of the Holy Spirit on us. Because if we go without the anointing that can only be obtained in Your very presence we will go with nothing to offer. We'll have the heart of the Father, we'll see the hungry, we'll see the naked, we'll see the poor but we won't be able to do anything if we haven't done this step first.

We need to do first things first! We need to come into Your House. We need to get Your heart. We need to get Your strategy. We need to get Your anointing. Then we will be propelled out into the End Time Harvest, and we will join You, and we will be in sync with You and with what You are doing in the Earth at this time. So Lord I just pray grace over us, grace over us, grace over us that we would see what You're doing at this time and that this is important, this is so, so important.

Appendix II
Recommended Reading

The Tabernacle of David and the House of Prayer

The Tabernacle of David by Kevin J. Conner

God's Favorite House by Tommy Tenny

The Power of His Presence by Graham Truscott

Red Moon Rising: how 24-7 prayer is awakening a generation by Peter Greig, Dave Roberts

The Establishment by J. Scott Husted

Worship

After God's Own Heart by Mike Bickle

The Pleasures of Loving God by Mike Bickle

The Singing God: Discover the Joy of Being Enjoyed by God by Sam Storms, Mike Bickle

The Sacred Romance by Brent Curtis & John Eldredge

The Power of Praise and Worship by Terry Law

To Know You More: Cultivating the Heart of the Worship Leader by Andy Park

The Unquenchable Worshipper by Matt Redman

Heart of the Artist, The by Rory Noland

The Worship Warrior: Finding the Power to Overcome by Chuck D. Pierce, John Dickson

Unceasing Worship: Biblical Perspectives on Worship and the Arts by Harold M. Best

Extravagant Worship: Holy, Holy, Holy Is the Lord God Almighty Who Was and Is, and Is to Come by Darlene Zschech

Enter The Worship Circle by Ben Pasley

A Heart of Worship by Boschman

Worship Him by Fuschia Pickett

The Power of Praise by Judson Cornwall

The Air I Breathe: Worship As a Way of Life by Louie Giglio

Facing The Wall by Don Potter

The Power of Prophetic Worship by David Swan

For The Audience of One by Mike Pilavachi

The Witness of Worship by Norm Strauss

The Lost Glory by David Markee

Sound of Heaven Symphony of Earth by Ray Hughes

Singing the Scriptures by Julie Meyer

Intercession

Praying The Bible by Wesley Campbell

Kneeling on the Promises: Birthing God's Purposes Through Prophetic Intercession by Jim W. Goll, Cindy Jacobs

The Lost Art of Intercession by Jim W. Goll

Reese Howells, Intercessor by Norman Grubb

Prophetic Intercession by Barbara Wentroble

The Breaker Anointing by Yoder

Watchman Prayer by Dutch Sheets

Bridal Intercession by Gary Wiens

Informed Intercession by George Otis Jr.

Releasing Heaven on Earth by Alistair Petrie

The Beginner's Guide to Intercession by Dutch Sheets

Intercessory Prayer: How God Can Use Your Prayers to Move Heaven and Earth by Dutch Sheets

Becoming a Prayer Warrior by Elizabeth Alves

Exodus Cry: Sounding a Prophetic Call to Strategic Prayer for Israel and the Jewish People Worldwide by Jim W. Goll

Intercession: Power and Passion to Shape History by Jim W. Goll

Crafted Prayer: The Joy Of Always Getting Your Prayers Answered by Graham Cooke

Operating in the Courts of Heaven by Robert Henderson

Unlocking Destinies from the Courts of Heaven by Robert Henderson

Revelation

Experiencing the Depths of Jesus Christ by Jeanne Guyonne

Developing Your Prophetic Gifting by Graham Cooke, Kevin Allan

Discerning of Spirits by Francis Frangipane

Dreams and Visions: Understanding Your Dreams and How God Can Use Them to Speak to You Today by Jane Hamon, Dutch Sheets

Receiving Divine Revelation by Fuschia Pickett

Your Sons and Your Daughters Shall Prophesy by Gentile

User Friendly Prophetic by Jack Deere

Developing Your Prophetic Gifting by Graham Cooke

When God Speaks: Receiving and Walking in Supernatural Revelation by Chuck D. Pierce, Rebecca Wagner Sytsema

You May All Prophesy by Steve Thompson

The Prophetic Ministry by Rick Joyner

The Seer by Jim Goll

The Beginner's Guide to the Gift of Prophecy by Jack Deere

Growing in the Prophetic by Mike Bickle, Michael Sullivant

Ecstatic Prophecy by Stacey Campbell

Mercy & Justice

Heavenly Man by Brother Yun

Taking Our Cities for God by John Dawson

City of Joy by Dominique La Pierre

Doing Justice, Showing Mercy : Christian Action in Today's World by Vinita Hampton Wright

Justice, Mercy and Humility: The Papers of the Micah Network by Tim Chester

Send My Roots Rain: A Spirituality of Justice and Mercy by Megan McKenna

Urban Ministry: The Kingdom, the City, & the People of God by Harvie M. Conn, Manuel Ortiz

Completing Capitalism by Bruno Roche and Jay Jakub

The Destiny of Nations by J. Scott Husted

Glory, Signs & Wonders

When Heaven Invades Earth by Bill Johnson

Power Evangelism by John Wimber

The Faith Factor: Proof of the Healing Power of Prayer by Dale A. Matthews, Connie Clark

Derek Prince on Experiencing God's Power by Derek Prince

Power Healing by John Wimber

Surprised by the Power of the Spirit by Jack Deere

When the Spirit Comes With Power: Signs and Wonders Among God's People by John White

The Person & Work of the Holy Spirit by R. A. Torrey

Good Morning, Holy Spirit : by Benny Hinn

You Will Receive Power by William Law

The Anointing : by Benny Hinn

Filled with the Spirit: Understanding God's Power in Your Life by Joyce Meyer

The Power of Faith by Smith Wigglesworth

Fresh Power by Jim Cymbala

If You Want to Walk on Water, You've Got to Get Out of the Boat by John Ortberg

Elijahs Revolution: The Call to Passion and Sacrifice for Radical Change by Jim W. Goll, Lou Engle

Wasted on Jesus : Reaching for the Lover of Your Soul by Jim W. Goll, Mike Bickle

The Fasting Key: How You Can Unlock Doors to Spiritual Blessing by Mark Nysewander, Mike Bickle

Passion for Jesus by Mike Bickle

Pleasures Evermore: The Life-Changing Power of Enjoying God by Sam Storms

Visions Beyond the Veil by H.A. Baker

Revealing Heaven by Kat Kerr

Faith Under Fire by Andrew White

Working With Angels by Steven Brooks

Leadership in the House of Prayer

Team Values by Maxwell

The Divine Conspiracy by Willard

Soul Tsunami by Leonard Sweet

Can You Hear Me by Brad Jersak

Dangerous Wonder by Yaconelli

A Tale of Three Kings by Gene Edwards

The Emerging Church by Dan Kimball

Church in Emerging Culture: Five Perspectives by Leonard Sweet

The Next Move of God by Fuschia Pickett

God's Dream Team: A Call to Unity by Tommy Tenney

A Divine Alliance by Jim Laffoon

In Search of Authentic Faith : How Emerging Generations Are Transforming the Church
by Steve Rabey

Soul Salsa
by Leonard Sweet

The Story We Find Ourselves In: Further Adventures of a New Kind of Christian
by Brian D. McLaren

A Servant's Manual: Christian Leadership for Tomorrow
by Michael W. Foss

The Language Of Love: Hearing And Speaking The Language Of God by Graham Cooke

Pastors & Prophets : Protocol For Healthy Churches
by C. Peter Wagner

Leaving Laodicea: A Call to Spiritual Passion
by Jeanne Terrell, Mike Bickle

The New Apostolic Churches
by C. Peter Wagner

Apostles and Prophets: The Foundation of the Church
by C. Peter Wagner

Churchquake : The Explosive Dynamics of the New Apostolic Revolution by C. Peter Wagner

Leading Kingdom Movements by Mike Breen

Building the Kingdom Through Business by Bridget Adams and Manoj Raithatha

Funding Your Ministry by Scott Morton

How Christianity Changed the World by Alvin J. Schmidt

The Seven Spirits of God by J. Scott Husted

Beyond the Education Machine by J. Scott Husted

Appendix III
Notes on Research in the House of Prayer

Research in the House of Prayer
> Revelation plus research as foundation for strategic prayer
> Quantitative Plus Qualitative
> Information serving spirit
> Heart over data

Steps:
1. Establish Baseline data
    > Based on Qualitative and Quantitative Sources- keep references
2. Choose research "Threads" -three
    > Based on General prayer focus, details of ongoing revelation, leader and team choices
3. Follow Threads in multiple sources
    > Two or Three witnesses
    > Continuous tracking and gathering- keep references
4. Reporting
    > Reporting to group leader for continual tracking and refining of threads
    > Reporting to group, foundation stone for strategic prayer
    > Archiving- making a prayer binder
5. Continuing cycle- Refining threads, following threads in multiple sources, ongoing reporting…

Appendix IV

The House of Prayer Training School

Overview

The need is great to build a structure of training for the House of Prayer that is accessible to the average person, and flexible enough to meet individuals' needs. At the same time this training experience must meet the need of the House of Prayer to raise up qualified long-term team members, as well as leaders who will go out with the vision, knowledge and skills to establish the House of Prayer throughout the earth.

In order to meet these diverse needs, we have made the structures and requirements of the HOP Training School simple and clearly spelled out, and have personal mentor teachers leading every group. Class sizes are kept unusually small, at 12 or so students, to facilitate a mentorship environment with a relational basis. To make it flexible we have structured it as multiple modules with choices of groups. Each student must show the maturity to be somewhat self-directed under the guidance of a group mentor for each module, able to complete a handful of simple requirements including a project. To keep it personalized, flexible and engaging, there are choices of readings and a great range of choices for projects which all follow a simple guideline.

The initial phase of the HOP Training School is a one-year program, or could be completed over a longer period. The student who wishes to complete the school in a year will take three modules every three months: the introductory module, and then a choice among the three core modules and the rest that may be available at any given time. The requirements of the basic course add up to nine modules in all.

Challenge Interview
We have built into the HOP Training School the option for a challenge interview with the module leader for anyone who feels they have the knowledge and experience to satisfy any specific module. Successful completion of the challenge interview will result in credit for the course. It is possible for those with a suitable combination of knowledge and experience in the given area to more than fulfill the criteria of the challenge interview.

Mentorship Groups
The initial experience is an orientation lead in a mentorship group format by HOP Training School pastoral staff. The rest of the modules are led by regular HOP members qualified to mentor and teach in the given area. Every new member, therefore, is initially mentored by the pastoral team, and then the mentoring responsibility is shared by regular team members with pastoral help and direction.

Each regular module is conducted in the atmosphere of a mentorship group with connection to fellow students and the mentor/instructor. This setting encourages a rich atmosphere of exploration, synthesis and creativity with much discussion and dialogue as we interact amongst the group and with curriculum materials. Classes will include reading and discussion, various kinds of interaction around core materials, and the development of group and individual projects. Connecting these experiences with hands-on involvement in the House of Prayer makes this a unique and dynamic learning opportunity.

Spiritual Life and Discipline

The House of Prayer Training School seeks to be a Spiritual

Community: a community of believers who desire to live out the two greatest commandments, Love above all toward the great heart of Jesus, and Love toward our brothers (Matt. 22:37-39). As such there are some minimum expectations for students to live a life of diligence and holiness. Students have the opportunity to be fully integrated into the life of The House of Prayer. This privilege calls us to the necessity of a clean walk before God in order not to open ourselves up to severe levels of spiritual warfare.

The House of Prayer Training School and the Local Church

The House of Prayer is an inter-denominational worship and prayer ministry. It is not, in and of itself, a local church. We do, however, have a close relationship with the ministries of many local churches. Our desire is for our staff members and students of the school to be established and serving within a local church during their involvement with the House of Prayer. Regular relationship with and involvement in any local church is encouraged, and we have a number of churches in the area that are partnering with our vision. If you would like additional information on some of these local churches, please contact the school administrator.

Expectations and Values

Students of the HOP Training School are expected to maintain a high degree of personal integrity and conform to a Biblical standard of morality. As those who aspire to become leaders, self-discipline and self-maintenance are greatly encouraged and emphasized. We also have a high value for relationship, and believe that this is the container given to us by God in which we can support one another in order to walk out our life of holiness. To this end, students will be encouraged to walk in relational openness with their student mentor and mentorship group. Students should be responsible within this context not only to conduct their public lives in a manner worthy of the Gospel of Christ, but must regularly cultivate a life with God in the secret place through personal spiritual disciplines and submission to the sanctifying influence of the Holy Spirit.

Admissions Policies and Procedures

The House of Prayer Training School seeks applicants who have a heart to learn and live the emerging House of Prayer paradigm, and to plant it in the earth. As such, applicants must have experienced a genuine conversion to the Lord Jesus Christ and be passionately committed to a life that will honor Him in all things. Admission to The House of Prayer Training School is open to all qualified individuals regardless of fellowship or denominational affiliation. The House of Prayer Training School is open to believers without regard to race, color, national or ethnic origin, gender, or physical handicap.

Applicants must satisfy the following requirements to be considered for acceptance into the school:

1. Minimally, potential students should normally be at least 18 years of age, have been a Christian for at least one year and begun to walk in spiritual discipline. A steady walk of discipleship with Christ or previous completion of a discipleship program is highly recommended.

2. A completed application form.

3. A pastoral recommendation form completed by a church leader who knows you well enough to address issues related to your Christian commitment, character, giftings, abilities, weaknesses, and lifestyle.

4. A personal recommendation form completed by a non-family member who can speak to your suitability as a student at The House of Prayer Training School.

5. A $25.00 non-refundable application fee.

All of the above materials must be received before your application will be processed for consideration. A letter of acceptance or non-acceptance will normally be mailed within two weeks of the receipt of all the material.

Applications will be received for consideration at any time. Enrollment in the school will begin at the starting date of the next open trimester. Your letter of acceptance will contain information on the dates of the next open trimester, or direct inquiries to the school director in order to obtain further information.

Normally, a student should have all materials mailed or faxed at least **45 days** before expected enrollment to insure enough time for the student to make appropriate housing arrangements. International students should allow at least 90 days. **All students are responsible for their own accommodations.** Initial arrangements can be made with school contact person by mail, email, phone or fax.

Weekly Time Requirements
2 hrs classroom per class
2 hrs reading per class
1-2 hrs project work (flexible) per class
20 hrs practicum overall full time, 12 hrs part time
2 hrs service

Each module is structured in three components over the 12 week quarter: 24 hrs. of Classroom and 10-15 hrs. reading, 220 hrs. Practicum, 20 hrs. project work, and 24 hrs. service.

Schedule
1 year program, with second year focusing on practical ministry

training in the planning stages. Modules in three 12-week trimesters. There will be three modules running concurrently initially.

- First trimester:

-Intro to the House Of Prayer
-Intercession module
- Research in the HOP

- Second trimester:

-Worship module
-Prophetic module
-Extreme Faith I
* Certificate in HOP Practice

- Third trimester:

-Leadership
-Extreme Faith II
-Mercy & Justice
* Certificate in HOP Leadership

Modules and Content

Introduction: The Tabernacle of David and the House of Prayer
-Classroom Studies (outline):
    -What is the House of Prayer? (Mike Bickel, Husted)
    -Foundations of intimacy (Noel Alexander, Patricia King, Husted)
    -The HOP and the strategic model (HOP Values, Cindy Jacobs)
    -The Three Strand Cord (Husted)
    -Priesthood model: Dynamics of every function, teams (Husted)
    -Intro to Worship (Husted)
    -Intro to Intercession (Husted)
    -Intro to Revelation and the prophetic (Husted, Campbell)
    -Personal Wholeness (Set Free, intro to listening prayer)
-3 Books from booklist on foundations of HOP
-Practicum in War Room
-1 project on the role of the House of Prayer in the earth

Intercession Module
-Classroom studies and mentoring (King, Alexander, Jacobs)
-3 Books from booklist on foundations of Intercession
-Intercession practicum in HOP
-1 project on the role of Intercession in the House of Prayer

Research Module
-Mentoring and classroom study in research processes
-Take up a research topic for a HOP project/session
-Project is research binder on prayer topic

Worship Module
-Classroom studies and mentoring (Wimber, Bickle, King)
-3 Books from booklist on foundations of worship
-Worship practicum in HOP
-1 project on the role of worship in the House of Prayer

Revelation (Prophetic) Module
-Classroom studies and mentoring (Chris Vallotton)
-3 Books from booklist on foundations of revelation
-Revelation practicum in HOP
-1 project on the role of revelation in the House of Prayer

Extreme Living I: Glory, Signs & Wonders

-Classroom studies and mentoring (King, Dew Healing Prayer model, Dew Deliverance model, World Missions Curriculum)

-3 Books from booklist on Glory, Signs and Wonders
-Prayer and prophetic outreach, practicum in HOP, possible involvement in healing rooms, Healing Gates, Father Heart ministries

-1 project based on practicum

Leadership in the House of Prayer
-Classroom studies and mentoring (Wagner, Deere, Pelton, Willard)

-3 Books from booklist on leadership in the new paradigm
-Practicum is to develop and lead a project or session in the House of Prayer
-1 project based on practicum experience

Extreme Living II: Faith, Community & Kingdom Finances

-Classroom studies and mentoring (Hill & Pitts, World Missions curriculum, FOTB Ministry Finances Curriculum)

-3 Books from booklist on Faith, Community & Kingdom Finances
-Practicum: practicum in HOP
-1 project: develop a vision, faith and finances strategy -- complete initial stages

Mercy & Justice Module
-Classroom studies and mentoring (Pullinger, Bromley, World Missions Curriculum)
-3 Books from booklists on Mercy and Justice
-Practicum: an outreach project, practicum in HOP
-1 project on the House of Prayer and Mercy & Justice

Module Projects
Every module requires the completion of a project. Due to the participatory and creative nature of the House of Prayer, projects will vary according to the module; they may be pursued individually or with a group, and have a wide choice of formats. The basic project guideline: Any communication or representation that is documented and observable, and that combines and expresses themes from the books and resources, themes from the classroom mentorship groups, experiences from the practicum, and a meaningful level of personal response. This means that students may pick, construct, or dream up their module project based around their individual gifts, interests and purposes.

Project Suggestions:

-a paper
-a teaching
-a dance with Q&A
-a video
-a verbal report
-a collection of artwork with presentation, Q&A
-a collection of songs with Q&A
-a collection of poetry with Q&A
-a collection of stories
-a PowerPoint slideshow
-a photo essay with presentation, Q&A
- a prophetic portfolio with reflections
-plan and lead an event
-a personal interview
-an article
-a news story
-a speech
-a sermon
-build a model with presentation
-a set of diagrams with presentation
*any project that would fulfill the guideline, arranged with the group leader!

J. Scott Husted Ph.D. is an author, editor, minister and Professor of Education living and working in Seoul, South Korea. Together with his wife Dionne, and an international team, they bring education, community development and spiritual outreach to tribal groups around the Pacific Rim. They have a passion for the establishment of the House of Prayer, the plight of children at risk around the world, and raising up a new generation of leaders with a passion for the kingdom of God. For more information go to: www.ringoffirehop.org.

Other Books written or edited by J. Scott Husted

Beyond the Education Machine

The Seven Spirits of God

The Destiny of Nations

The Meat From the Mystics Series

The World of Adventure Series

The Pacific Gates University Press Series

All of these and more can be found at:

www.bibliographypress.com